Deviant Love

SIGMUND FREUD

Deviant Love

Translated by SHAUN WHITESIDE

GREAT LOVES

PENGUIN BOOKS

Published by the Penguin Group
Penguin Books Ltd, 80 Strand, London WC2R ORL, England
Penguin Group (USA) Inc., 375 Hudson Street, New York, New York 10014, USA
Penguin Group (Canada), 90 Eglinton Avenue East, Suite 700, Toronto, Ontario, Canada M4P 2Y3
(a division of Pearson Penguin Canada Inc.)
Penguin Ireland, 25 St Stephen's Green, Dublin 2, Ireland
(a division of Penguin Books Ltd)
Penguin Group (Australia), 250 Camberwell Road, Camberwell, Victoria 3124, Australia
(a division of Pearson Australia Group Pty Ltd)
Penguin Books India Pvt Ltd, 11 Community Centre, Panchsheel Park, New Delhi – 110 017, India
Penguin Group (NZ), 67 Apollo Drive, Rosedale, North Shore 0632, New Zealand
(a division of Pearson New Zealand Ltd)
Penguin Books (South Africa) (Pty) Ltd, 24 Sturdee Avenue,
Rosebank, Johannesburg 2196, South Africa

Penguin Books Ltd, Registered Offices: 80 Strand, London WC2R ORL, England

www.penguin.com

Drei Abhandlungen zur Sexualtheorie first published 1905 (Leipzig, Vienna)
'Über einen besonderen Typus Objektwahl beim Manne' first published in 1910 (Leipzig, Vienna) in
Jahrbuch für psychoanalytische und psychopathologische Forschungen
'Das Tabu der Virginität' first published in 1918 (Leipzig) in Sigmund Freud, *Sammlung kleiner
Schriften zur Neurosenlehre*
' "Ein Kind wird geschlagen": Beitrag zur Kenntnis der Enstellung sexueller Perversionen'
first published in 1919 (Leipzig) in *Internationale Zeitschrift für ärztliche Psychoanalyse*
'Überdie wiebliche Sexualität' first published in 1931 (Leipzig) in *Internationale Zeitschrift
für ärztliche Psychoanalyse*
Published in Penguin Classics as *The Psychology of Love* 2006
This selection published in Penguin Books 2007

1

Sigmund Freud's German texts collected in *Gesammelte Werke* (1940–52) copyright © Imago
Publishing Co., Ltd, London, 1905, 1908, 1910, 1912, 1918, 1919, 1931
Translation and editorial matter copyright © Shaun Whiteside, 2006
All rights reserved

Typeset by Rowland Phototypesetting Ltd, Bury St Edmunds, Suffolk
Printed in England by Clays Ltd, St Ives plc

978-0-141-03286-3

Contents

Sigmund Freud (1856–1939) was born in Moravia. Between the ages of four and eighty-two his home was in Vienna, but in 1938 Hitler's invasion forced him to seek asylum in London where he died the following year. His career began with several years of brilliant work on the anatomy and physiology of the nervous system. He was almost thirty when, after a period of study under Charcot in Paris, his interests first turned to psychology; and after ten years of clinical work in Vienna (at first in collaboration with Breuer, an older colleague) he invented what was to become psychoanalysis. This began simply as a method of treating neurotic patients through talking, but it quickly grew into an accumulation of knowledge about the workings of the mind in general. Freud was thus able to demonstrate the development of the sexual instinct in childhood, and largely on the basis of an examination of dreams, arrived at his fundamental discovery of the unconscious forces that influence our everyday thoughts and actions. His illuminating discussions of the ways in which sexuality is always psychosexuality – that there is no sexuality without fantasy, conscious or unconscious – have changed the ways we think about erotic life and the psychology of love.

Concerning a Particular Type of Object-choice in Men

In the past, we have left it to the poets to depict for us the 'conditions of love', according to which people make their object-choices, and how they reconcile the demands of their fantasy with reality. Poets have certain qualities that enable them to solve such a task, in particular a great sensitivity in the perception of hidden mental impulses in others, and the courage to make their own unconscious speak. But one factor reduces the value of their communications. Poets are bound to the condition of achieving intellectual and aesthetic pleasure as well as certain emotional effects, and for that reason they cannot represent the stuff of reality unaltered, but are obliged to isolate fragments of it, dissolve obstructive connections, soften the whole and fill any gaps. These are the privileges of what is known as 'poetic licence'. In addition, they can express only a small degree of interest in the origin and development of such mental states, which they describe as complete. As a result, however, it is inevitable that science should use a heavier hand, bringing a smaller gain in pleasure, when dealing with the same material, whose poetic treatment has been delighting people for thousands of years. These observations may also serve to justify a strictly scientific treatment of human erotic life. Science is, in fact, the most complete renunciation of the pleasure principle of which our psychical work is capable.

During psychoanalytic treatment one has ample opportunity to glean impressions from the erotic life of neurotics, while at the same time bearing in mind that one has also observed or experienced similar behaviour among people of average health, or even among exceptional people. When favourable material permits the accumulation of impressions, individual types clearly emerge. Here I should first like to describe one such type of male object-choice, both because it presents itself as a series of 'conditions of love', whose co-existence is not comprehensible – in fact it is frankly alarming – and because it permits simple psycho-analytical explanation.

1) The first of these conditions of love should be identified as being effectively specific; as soon as one comes across it, one can seek the presence of the other characteristics of this type. One might refer to it as the condition of the '*damaged third*'; its content leads the person concerned never to choose as a love object a woman who is free, a girl or a single woman, but only a woman to whom another man can apply property rights, whether as husband, fiancé or friend. In some cases this condition proves so potent that the same woman can at first be ignored or even despised as long as she does not belong to anyone, while she immediately becomes the object of passionate love as soon as she enters one of the aforementioned relationships with another man.

2) The second condition is perhaps less constant,

but none the less striking. This type is only fulfilled by its coincidence with the first, while the first also appears to occur in great frequency on its own. According to this second condition, the modest and unimpeachable woman never exerts the charm that raises her to become a love object; that charm will only be exerted by a woman who has somehow acquired a bad sexual reputation, and about whose fidelity and dependability there might be some doubt. This latter characteristic may vary significantly, from the faint shadow cast upon the reputation of a wife who is not disinclined to flirt to the openly polygamous conduct of a coquette or an adept in the art of love; at any rate, it is something of this kind that men belonging to our type cannot do without. To put it a little coarsely, we might call this condition 'love of whores'.

Just as the first condition gives rise to the satisfaction of agonistic and hostile impulses against the man from whom one is seizing the beloved woman, the second condition, which requires the woman to behave in some way like a prostitute, is related to the activation of *jealousy*, which seems to be a need for lovers of this type. Only if these men can be jealous does the passion reach its peak and the woman attain her full value, and the men never miss an opportunity to experience these most intense sensations. Curiously, the jealousy is directed not at the rightful owner of the beloved, but at newly arriving strangers who might cast suspicion upon the beloved. In extreme cases, the lover shows no desire to possess the woman for himself alone, and appears to feel entirely at ease in the triangular relationship. One of my patients, who had suffered terribly as a result of his lady's indiscretions, had no objections to her getting married, in fact he did all he could to encourage it. Then for years he never showed a sign of jealousy. Another typical case, however, had in his earliest love relationships been very jealous of the husband, and had demanded that the lady cease marital intercourse with him; in his many later relationships, however, he behaved like others and no longer saw the legitimate husband as a disturbance.

The following paragraphs do not describe the conditions required of the love object, but the behaviour of the lover towards the object of his choice.

3) In normal love-life the value of the woman is determined by her sexual integrity, and reduced by her approach to the character of the prostitute. So it seems to be a striking deviation from the normal if lovers of our type treat women with this character as *love objects of the highest value*. Relationships of love with these women are carried on by the greatest psychical expenditure, to the point of consuming all other interests; these women are the only people one could love, and the requirement of fidelity that the subject imposes on himself is renewed each time it can be broken down in reality. Within these traits of relationships of love we can see with extreme clarity the *compulsive* character that is always to a certain degree a part of passionate love. But the fidelity and intensity of the connection do not allow us to infer that such a love relationship fills the erotic life of the person in question, or even that it occurs only once. On the contrary, passions of

this kind are repeated, with the same curious qualities – one the precise image of the other – several times during the life of a man belonging to this type; indeed, depending upon outward conditions, such as a change of residence or surroundings, love objects can be replaced so often that they finally form *a long series*.

4) The most surprising thing for the observer, among lovers of this type, is the manifest tendency to '*rescue*' the loved one. The man is convinced that the woman needs him, that without him she will lose all moral control and rapidly descend to a deplorable level. So he is saving her by not letting her out of his sight. In individual cases, the intention of saving can be justified by the invocation of sexual unreliability and the socially threatened position of the lover; but it appears no less clearly where such supports are absent in reality. One man of this type, who was able to win his ladies through artful seduction and a subtle dialectics, spared himself no efforts in the relationship to keep his chosen one on the path of 'virtue' by means of self-penned treatises.

If we were to consider all the individual traits of the picture described here – the condition decreeing that the woman should not be free, or that she should behave like a prostitute, the high value placed upon the woman in question, the need for jealousy, the fidelity that is none the less compatible with a long series of objects, and the intention of saving the woman – we would consider it unlikely that they could all derive from a single source. And yet, if we consider the life histories of the people in question, immersing ourselves psychoanalytically in them, we will easily reach such a conclusion. The curious definition of object-choice, and the strange amorous behaviour, have the same psychical source as in the erotic life of normal people; they arise out of the infantile fixation of tenderness upon the mother and represent one of the outcomes of that fixation. Normal love-life contains only a few residual traits which unmistakably reveal the maternal model of the object-choice, such as the love of young men for more mature women; the libido was detached from the mother relatively quickly. In our type, on the other hand, the libido has lingered so long with the mother, even after the onset of puberty, that the love objects chosen subsequently possess the imprint of maternal characteristics, and all become easily recognizable maternal surrogates. Here we might make the comparison with the skull formation of the new-born; after a protracted birth the child's skull must represent the cast of the maternal pelvic canal.

Our task now is to justify the idea that the characteristic traits of our type, both the conditions of love and amorous behaviour, really do emerge from the maternal constellation. This might be most easily accomplished in relation to the first condition – the woman's unfreedom – or the condition of the damaged third party. One sees immediately that for a child who has grown up in a family, the fact that the mother belongs to the father becomes an inseparable part of the maternal essence, and the injured third party is none other than the father. Equally easy to identify as being related to the infantile connection is the supplementary trait of over-valuation: the loved one is the only one, she is irreplaceable. For no one has more than one mother, and the relationship with the mother is based on an unrepeatable event that is beyond any doubt.

If the love objects in our type are above all supposed to be mother surrogates, the formation of series, which so directly contradicts the condition of fidelity, becomes comprehensible. Psychoanalysis also teaches us, with reference to other examples, that the notion of something irreplaceable in the unconscious often announces its presence by breaking down into an infinite series – infinite because no surrogate possesses the required satisfaction. So the insatiable desire to ask questions, seen in children at a certain age, is explained by the fact that they have only a single question to ask, and it is one that they cannot utter. Similarly, the loquacity of some neurotically damaged people is produced by the pressure of a secret that demands to be communicated, but which, in the face of all temptation, they will still not betray.

On the other hand, the second condition of love, requiring the chosen object's resemblance to a prostitute, seems energetically to resist inference from the mother complex. To the adult's conscious thought the mother tends to appear a person of unimpeachable moral purity, and hardly anything can be so insulting, if it comes from without, or so tormenting if it comes from within, as doubt of this characteristic in her. This relationship of the keenest opposition between the 'mother' and the 'whore', however, will prompt us to examine the unconscious relationship between these two complexes, since we learned long ago that what is split in two in consciousness joins into one in the unconscious. Our investigation then leads us back to the time when the boy begins to acquire a more complete knowledge of sexual relationships between adults, in the years just before puberty. At this point, brutal pieces of information, tending undisguisedly to provoke contempt and rebellion, familiarize him with the mystery of the sexual life, destroying the authority of adults, which proves to be irreconcilable with the revelation of their sexual activity. The greatest impression made on the new initiate is in the connection between this information and his own parents. That relationship is often categorically rejected, with words along the lines: 'Maybe your parents and other people do things like that with each other, but with my parents it's quite impossible.'

It is a rarely absent corollary to 'sexual enlightenment' that, at the same time, the boy becomes aware of the existence of certain women who perform the sexual act in return for money, and who are for that reason universally despised. This contempt must be far from the boy's mind; all he can muster for these unfortunates is a mixture of longing and horror, once he knows that they could introduce him, too, into sexual life, which he hitherto considered the exclusive preserve of the 'grown-ups'. If he can then no longer maintain the doubt that his parents are an exception to the ugly norms of sexual activity, he can tell himself with the perfect reasoning of the cynic that the difference between the mother and the whore is not so great after all, that they basically do the same thing. The explanations have in fact awoken trace memories of the impressions and desires of his early childhood, and have reactivated certain psychical impulses on the basis of those traces. The boy begins to desire his mother in a new way, and begins to hate his father again, as a rival standing in the way of his desire; he comes, as we say, under the control of the Oedipus complex. He does not forget this about his mother and considers it an act of infidelity that she has bestowed the favour of sexual intercourse not upon him but upon his father. If these impulses do not pass quickly, they inevitably lead to fantasies whose content is the mother's sexual activity in the most diverse forms, and the tension accompanying them is particularly easily resolved in the act of masturbation. As a result of the constant collaboration of these two driving motives, desirability and the desire for revenge, fantasies of the mother's infidelity are by far the most common; the lover with whom the mother commits infidelity almost always bears the traits of the subject's own self, or more properly those traits in an idealized form, as an adult and elevated to the level of the father. What I have described elsewhere as the 'family romance' (or 'family saga') encompasses the various formations of this fantasy activity and its interweaving with the various egoistic interests of this age. Once we have understood this piece of mental development, however, we can no longer find it contradictory and incomprehensible that the condition of the lover's resemblance to a prostitute is derived directly from the mother complex. The type of masculine erotic life that we have described bears the traces of this evolution, and can be simply understood as a fixation on the boy's pubertal fantasies, which have later found an outlet in the reality of life. It is not difficult to assume that the eagerly practised masturbation of the years of puberty has made its contribution to the fixation of those fantasies.

The tendency to *save* the loved one seems to have only a loose and superficial connection with these fantasies, which have come to dominate real erotic life, and one that can be reduced to a conscious explanation. The loved one puts herself in danger by being inclined towards inconstancy and infidelity, so it is understandable that the lover should try to protect her against those dangers by guarding her virtue and working against her bad inclinations. In the meantime the study of screen memories, fantasies and nocturnal dreams reveals that what we have here is an eminently successful 'rationalization' of an unconscious motive, which might be equated with a highly successful secondary elaboration in the dream. In fact, the *saving motive* has a meaning and history of its own and is an independent descendant of the mother complex or, more correctly, the parent complex. When the child hears that he *owes* his life to his parents, that his mother '*gave him life*', affectionate impulses unite with impulses struggling towards adult manhood, towards independence; these yield the desire to return this gift to the parents, to give them something of equal value. It is as though the boy wished to say in defiance: I need nothing from my father, I want to give him back everything I have cost him. He then forms the fantasy of *rescuing his father from life-threatening danger*, thus leaving things even between them. In many cases this fantasy is displaced on to the emperor, the king or some other great man, and after this displacement has taken place it becomes capable of reaching consciousness, and is even usable to the poet. As applied to the father, the defiant meaning of the rescue fantasy is greatly predominant; when applied to the mother it generally assumes its affectionate meaning. The mother has given life to the child, and that unique gift cannot easily be replaced with something of equal value. With one of those small changes of meaning facilitated in the unconscious – and which we might, for example, equate with the flowing of one concept into another in the consciousness – the rescue of the mother assumes the meaning: give or make her a child, of course a child as one is oneself. The distance from the original meaning of rescue is not terribly great, and the shift in meaning is not arbitrary. One's mother has given one a life, one's own, and in return one is giving her another life, that of a child, highly similar to one's own self. The son proves his gratitude by wishing to have a son with his mother, who is equal to himself; in the rescue fantasy, that is to say, he identifies completely with his father. All drives, whether affectionate, grateful, lustful, defiant or self-glorifying, are satisfied by the single desire *to be his own father*. The moment of danger is not lost in the change of meaning; the act of birth, in fact, is the very first danger from which one was rescued by one's mother's efforts. Equally, birth is the first life-threatening danger, since it is the model of everything that will afterwards cause us to feel fear, and the experience of birth has probably left us with the affective expression that we call fear. The Macduff of Scottish legend, who was not born of his mother, but cut from his mother's womb, was unacquainted with fear for the same reason.

The ancient interpreter of dreams, Artemidorus, was certainly right in claiming that a dream changes its meaning according to the person of the dreamer. According to the rules for the expression of unconscious thoughts, 'rescue' can vary its meaning, according to whether it is fantasized by a woman or a man. It can mean either: to make a child = to cause to be born (for the man) or: to have a child oneself (for the woman).

Particularly when they are associated with water, the various meanings of rescue in dreams and fantasies make themselves clearly apparent. If a man in a dream rescues a woman from water, it means he is turning her into a mother, which means, according to the above reflections, he makes her his own mother. If a woman rescues someone else (a child) from the water, she is thus declaring herself, like the king's daughter in the legend of Moses, to be the mother who brought him into the world.

Sometimes the rescue fantasy may have an affectionate meaning when it involves the father. In that case it seeks to express the desire to have the father as a son, that is, to have a son who resembles the father. Because of all these relationships between the rescue motif and the parent complex, the tendency to rescue the loved one constitutes an essential trait of the type of love described here.

I do not deem it necessary to justify my working method, which, as in my presentation of *anal eroticism*, at first stresses extreme and sharply circumscribed types from the observed material. In both cases there are far more individuals in whom these traits can only be identified in smaller numbers or in an indistinct form, and it is obvious that only the interpretation of the entire context in which these types are received makes possible their proper evaluation.

(1910)

The Sexual Deviations

When biologists discuss the sexual needs of men and animals, they assume the existence of a 'sexual drive', following the analogy of the drive to seek food – hunger. The vernacular lacks a term corresponding to the word 'hunger'; for this purpose, science uses the word 'libido'.

Popular opinion has quite particular notions of the nature and properties of this sexual drive. It is supposed to be absent from childhood, and to set in with the maturing process of puberty, when it finds expression in the irresistible attraction that one sex exerts upon the other, and its goal is supposed to be sexual union or at least the actions that lie on the route to that union.

But we have every reason to see this account as a very unfaithful depiction of reality; if we take a closer look at it, it proves to be abundant in errors, imprecision and hasty judgements.

Let us introduce two terms: if we call the person exuding the sexual attraction the *sexual object*, and the action towards which the drive urges the *sexual goal*, scientifically examined experience reveals numerous deviations in relation to both sexual object and sexual goal, whose relationship towards the accepted norm calls for detailed examination.

1) Deviations Regarding the Sexual Object

The popular theory of the sexual drive is most beautifully expressed by the poetic fable of the division of the human being into two halves – man and woman – which seek to reunite in love. So it seems to come as a great surprise to hear that there are men whose sexual object is not women but men, and women whose sexual object is not men but women. Such people are called 'countersexual' or, more exactly, inverts, and the fact is that of *inversion*. The number of such people is very considerable, although it is difficult to arrive at precise figures.

A) Inversion

(BEHAVIOUR OF INVERTS)

The people in question behave in different ways in different contexts.

a) They may be *absolutely* inverted, which is to say that their sexual object can only be of the same sex, while the opposite sex is never the object of their sexual longing, but leaves them cold or even provokes sexual repulsion in them. As men they are then, by virtue of this repulsion, incapable of performing the normal sex act, or else they lack all pleasure in its performance.

b) They may be *amphigenically inverted* (psychosexually hermaphroditic), that is, their sexual object can belong equally well to the same as to the other sex; so their inversion lacks the character of exclusivity. *c*) They may be *occasionally* inverted, that is, under certain external conditions, chief among which are a lack of access to the normal sexual object and imitation, they can take a person of the same sex as their sexual object, and feel satisfaction in the sexual act with that person.

Inverts also demonstrate different attitudes in their assessment of the special nature of their sexual instinct. Some take inversion perfectly for granted, just as a normal person will take the direction of his libido to be quite natural, and keenly stress their equality with normal people. But others reject the fact of their inversion and perceive it as a morbid compulsion.

Other variations apply to relations over time. The characteristic nature of an individual's inversion either dates from as far back as his memory goes, or has only made itself apparent at a particular time before or after puberty. The characteristic is either maintained throughout the whole of life, or subsides for periods of time, or represents an episode on the path towards normal development; indeed it is sometimes manifested only late in life, after a long period of normal sexual activity. A periodic vacillation between the normal and the inverted sexual object has also been observed. Of particular interest are those cases in which the libido changes its direction to move towards the inversion, after a painful experience with the normal sexual object.

These different series of variations generally exist independently of one another. Where the most extreme form is concerned, for example, we might generally assume that the inversion has existed since very early on, and that the person feels himself to be at one with its peculiarity.

Many authors would refuse to assemble the cases enumerated here into a unit, preferring to stress the differences between these groups rather than what they have in common, and this has to do with their preferred judgement of inversion. But while there may be considerable justification for separating out certain cases, there is no mistaking the fact that all intermediate stages are to be found in abundance, so that series might be said to form of their own accord.

(CONCEPT OF INVERSION)

The first concept of inversion consisted in the notion that it was an innate sign of nervous degeneracy, and was in harmony with the fact that medical observers first encountered it among patients suffering from, or appearing to suffer from, nervous disorders. This characteristic contains two features that should be judged independently of each other: innateness and degeneracy.

(DEGENERACY)

The term 'degeneracy' is vulnerable to all those objections that can be raised against the unselective use of the word in general. None the less it has become customary to impute to degeneracy any expression of an illness that is not precisely traumatic or infectious in origin. According to Magnan's categorization of degenerates, even the most excellent general formation of neural functioning need not exclude the concept of degeneracy. In such circumstances we might wonder what use and what new content the diagnosis of 'degeneracy' might possess, if any. It seems to make more sense not to speak of degeneracy:

1) where several serious deviations from the norm do not coincide;

2) where the capacity for achievement and existence do not in general appear to be seriously damaged.

That inverts are not degenerates in this justified sense emerges from several facts:

1) inversion is encountered amongst people who show no other serious deviations from the norm;

2) the same is true of people whose capacities are not impeded, and who are distinguished by particularly high levels of intellectual development and ethical culture;

3) if we ignore those patients whom we have encountered in our own medical experience and attempt to encompass a further range of views, in two directions we run into facts which prohibit us from viewing inversion as a sign of degeneracy:

a) we must stress that inversion was a common phenomenon, almost an institution, entrusted with important functions, among ancient peoples at the peak of their culture;

b) we find it to be uncommonly widespread among many savage and primitive peoples, despite the fact that we usually restrict the concept of degeneracy to high civilization (I. Bloch); even among the civilized peoples of Europe, climate and race have the most powerful influence on the distribution and assessment of inversion.

(INNATENESS)

Understandably, the innate source of inversion has only been suggested for the first and most extreme class of inverts, based on their assurance that they had never in their lives shown any other direction in their sexual drives. The very existence of the other two classes, particularly the third, is difficult to reconcile with the view of a congenital character. Hence the tendency among those who hold this view to separate the group of absolute inverts off from all others, leading to the abandonment of a universally valid understanding of inversion. This would mean that inversion had an innate characteristic in one series of cases; in others it could have come about in a different way.

The antithesis to this view is that inversion is an *acquired* characteristic of the sexual drive. It is based on the idea that:

1) among many inverts (some of them absolute), an influential sexual impression early in life can be demonstrated, having the lasting consequence of an inclination towards homosexuality;

2) in many other cases it is possible to reveal the external encouraging and inhibiting influences of life that have led, sooner or later, to the fixation of the inversion

(exclusive intercourse with the same sex, comradeship in war, detention in prisons, dangers of heterosexual intercourse, celibacy, sexual weakness, etc.);

3) that the inversion can be abolished by hypnotic suggestion, which would be astonishing if the characteristic were innate.

From this point of view, it is possible to dispute the certainty of the occurrence of innate inversion in general. One might object (with Havelock Ellis) that a more precise examination of the cases claimed for innate inversion would probably also tend to reveal an experience in early childhood which defined the direction of the libido, one which has not been stored in the person's conscious memory, but which could be remembered by recourse to the appropriate influence. According to these authors, inversion could only be characterized as a frequently occurring variation of the sexual drive, which can be determined by a considerable number of external circumstances in an individual's life.

But the certainty apparently achieved in this way is defeated by the contrary observation that many people demonstrably undergo the same sexual influences (even in early adolescence: seduction, mutual masturbation) without being inverted in the process or remaining so in the long term. One is therefore obliged to assume that the innate–acquired opposition is either incomplete or does not fully account for the conditions involved in inversion.

(EXPLANATION OF INVERSION)

Neither the assumption that inversion is innate, nor that it is acquired, explains its essence. In the former case one must state what is innate about it if one is not to adopt the crudest explanation, that there is an innate link between a person's drive and a particular sexual object. In the other case the question arises of whether the diverse accidental influences alone adequately explain the acquisition of the inversions, and need no compliance from the individual to meet them. According to our earlier expositions, the denial of this latter element is not permissible.

(INVOCATION OF BISEXUALITY)

Popular opinion is contradicted by the reflections of Frank Lydstone, Kiernan and Chevalier, in their endeavour to explain the possibility of sexual inversion. According to this view, a person is held to be either a man or a woman. But science is aware of cases in which the sexual characteristics appear blurred, and sexual definition consequently becomes more difficult, first of all in the anatomical field. The genitals of such people combine male and female characteristics (hermaphroditism). In rare cases, the two sexual apparatuses are formed side by side (true hermaphroditism); in the most usual cases one finds atrophy on both sides.

What is significant about these abnormalities, however, is that they unexpectedly make it easier to understand the normal formation. A certain degree of anatomical hermaphroditism is actually part of the norm; all normally formed male or female individuals possess traces of the apparatus of the opposite sex, and these continue to exist either without a function as rudimentary organs, or have been reconstructed to assume other functions.

The understanding yielded by these long-known anatomical facts is that of an originally bisexual disposition, which changes in the course of its development into monosexuality, with small residues of the atrophied sex.

It seemed reasonable to transfer this understanding of inversion to the psychical sphere and see it in its deviant versions as the manifestation of a psychical hermaphroditism. For the resolution of this question, all that was required was a regular coincidence between inversion and the mental and somatic signs of hermaphroditism.

But this immediate expectation proves to be incorrect. We must not conceive such close relations between the assumed psychical and demonstrable anatomical hermaphroditism. What we find among inverts is frequently a reduction in the sexual drive in general (Havelock Ellis) and slight anatomical atrophy of the organs. Frequently, but by no means regularly or even predominantly. Thus we must concede that inversion and somatic hermaphroditism are entirely independent of one another.

In addition, great stress has been placed on the so-called secondary and tertiary sexual characteristics, and their accumulated occurrence among inverts (H. Ellis).

This is also true in many respects, but we should not forget that the secondary and tertiary sexual characteristics in general appear very frequently in the opposite sex, and thus produce suggestions of hermaphroditism without the sexual object being altered in the sense of an inversion.

Psychical hermaphroditism would gain substance if the inversion of the sexual object were at least accompanied by a parallel change in the other mental qualities, drives and character traits into those characteristic of the other sex. However, such a character inversion can only be expected with any regularity among inverted women, while in men inversion may be reconciled with the most complete mental masculinity. If we are determined to establish the idea of mental hermaphroditism, we must add that in various respects its manifestations reveal only a very small degree of reciprocal causality. The same is also true of somatic hermaphroditism: according to Halban, the atrophy of individual organs and secondary sexual characteristics appear fairly independently of one another.

The crudest form of the theory of bisexuality has been put forward by a spokesman for male inverts: a female brain in a male body. But we do not know what the characteristics of a 'female brain' might be. The substitution of the anatomical for the psychical problem is as futile as it is unjustified. Krafft-Ebing's attempt at an explanation seems to be more precisely put than that of Ulrichs, but is no different in its essentials: Krafft-Ebing says that the bisexual predisposition produces individual brain-centres that are just as male and female as the somatic sexual organs. These centres develop only during puberty, and mostly under the influence of glands that are independent of them within the sexual predisposition. We may, however, say the same of these male and female 'centres' as we do of the male and female brain. In addition, we do not even know whether we can assume that there are distinct points in the brain ('centres') as we can, for example, for language.

These discussions leave us with two thoughts: that a bisexual predisposition also has some bearing on inversion, although we do not know what that predisposition consists of beyond anatomical formation, and that these are disorders which affect the development of the sexual drive.

(SEXUAL OBJECT OF INVERTS)

The theory of psychical hermaphroditism assumes that the invert's sexual object is the opposite of a normal person's. According to this theory the male invert, like a woman, succumbs to the enchantment emanated by the male qualities of body and mind. He himself feels like a woman and seeks a man.

But however true this may be for large numbers of inverts, it is still a long way from revealing a general character of inversion. Beyond a doubt, a high proportion of male inverts have preserved the psychical character of masculinity, have relatively few secondary characteristics of the opposite sex, and actually seek female psychical traits in their sexual object. If this were not the case, we would be unable to understand why the male prostitutes available to the invert – today as in antiquity – copy women in all externals of clothing and posture; were this not the case, this imitation would surely insult the ideal of inverts. Among the ancient Greeks, among whom inverts included the most masculine of men, it is clear that it was not the masculine character of the boy but his physical similarity to women, along with his feminine mental qualities, such as shyness, reticence, a need to learn and to be helped, that fired the love of men. As soon as the boy became a man he ceased to be a sexual object for men, and in all likelihood became a lover of boys himself. So in this case, as in many others, the sexual object is not the same sex but the combination of both characteristics, the compromise, one might say, between one impulse that craves a man and another that craves a woman, with the body's permanent condition of maleness (the genitals) the reflection, so to speak, of the subject's own bisexual nature.

Less ambiguous are conditions among women, whereby active inverts most usually bear male somatic and mental characteristics and demand femininity in their sexual object, although even here a greater variety might appear on closer examination.

(SEXUAL GOAL OF INVERTS)

The important fact to bear in mind is that in inversion the sexual goal should by no means be considered uniform. Among men, intercourse *per anum* [anal intercourse] does not correspond to inversion; equally often, masturbation is the exclusive goal, and restrictions of the sexual goal – down to the mere outpouring of emotions – are even more frequent here than in heterosexual love. Among women, too, the sexual goals of inverts are highly diverse; among them, contact with the oral mucous membrane seems to be preferred.

(CONCLUSION)

We are not in a position to give a satisfactory explanation of the origin of inversion on the basis of this material, but we may observe that in the course of this investigation we have reached an insight that might be more significant to us than the solution of the task mentioned above. We are aware that we have considered the connection between sexual drive and sexual object to be deeper than it is. The experience of those cases which are considered abnormal tells us that a powerful bond exists between sexual drive and sexual object, and that we are in danger of overlooking it because of the uniformity of the normal arrangement, in which the drive itself appears to bring an innate object along with it. For this reason we tend to loosen the connection between drive and object in our minds. The sexual drive is probably at first independent of its object, and in all likelihood its origins do not lie in its object's attractions.

B) Sexually Immature People and Animals as Sexual Objects

While those people whose sexual objects do not belong to the normally appropriate sex, those whom we shall call inverts, may strike the observer as a collection of otherwise fully adequate individuals, the cases in which people who have not reached sexual maturity (children) are chosen as sexual objects immediately appear as individual aberrations. Only in exceptional cases are children the sole sexual objects; they usually attain this role if a cowardly individual, who has developed impotence, chooses them as a surrogate, or if an impulsive (urgent) drive can at that moment find no more suitable object. None the less, it casts a light on the nature of the sexual drive that it permits so much variation and such debasement of its object, something that hunger, which is far more energetic in its retention of its object, would only permit in extreme cases. A similar observation applies to sexual intercourse with animals, which is far from rare amongst rural people, in which sexual attraction goes beyond the boundaries of species.

For aesthetic reasons we would very much like to attribute these and other serious deviations of the sexual drive to the mentally ill, but we cannot do so. Experience teaches us that among the latter the observable disorders of the sexual drive are no different from those seen among healthy people, among entire races and social classes. Thus the sexual abuse of children occurs with extraordinary frequency among teachers and carers simply because they are presented with the best opportunity to abuse. The mentally ill only show the aberration in question in an intensified form or, very significantly, elevated to an exclusive role and replacing normal sexual satisfaction.

This very peculiar relationship between sexual variations and the range between health and mental disorder provides food for thought. I am inclined to the view that what needs to be explained is the fact that the impulses of sexual life are among those least effectively controlled by the higher activities of the mind. A person who is mentally abnormal in another context, in a social or ethical respect, will in my experience be regular in his sexual life. But there are many who are abnormal in their sexual life but who correspond in all other respects to the average, and who have personally played their part in the development of human civilization, the weak point of which is still sexuality.

The most general result of these discussions, however, would seem to be the insight that in a large number of conditions and among a surprisingly large number of individuals the nature and value of the sexual object are of secondary importance. The essential and constant feature of the sexual drive is clearly something else.

Sigmund Freud GmbH
Berggasse 19
1090 Wien
319 15 96

Rechnung: 409777/ 413549 vom 30.07.2013

| 1 Freud Deviant Love | 9,90 | 9,90 |
| 1 Freud The future of an | 9,90 | 9,90 |

Gesamtsumme: EUR 19,80

egeben Visa

nthaltene MwSt:	Netto:	MwSt:
10%:	18,00	1,80
20%:	0,00	0,00

Vielen Dank für Ihren Besuch!
Thank you for your visit!
http://www.freud-museum.at

2) Deviations Regarding the Sexual Goal

The normal sexual goal is generally supposed to be the union of the genitals in the act described as coitus, which leads to the release of sexual excitement (a satisfaction analogous to the sating of hunger). But even in the most normal sexual procedure we can see the first signs of something which, when fully developed, will lead to the aberrations described as *perversions*. Indeed, certain intermediate relationships towards the sexual object (along the path towards coitus), such as touching and looking at the object, are acknowledged as temporary sexual goals. On the one hand these activities are themselves connected with pleasure, while on the other they intensify the excitement that should lead to the achievement of the final sexual goal. One of these contacts in particular, the mutual contact of the mucous membrane of the lips, has also achieved high sexual value as a kiss among many peoples (including the most highly civilized), although the parts of the body in question are not part of the sexual apparatus, but in fact form the entrance to the alimentary canal. Here, then, we have elements which link perversions to normal sexual life, and which are applicable to their organization. The perversions are either a) anatomical *transgressions* of those areas of the body destined for sexual union or b) a *lingering* over the intermediate relations to the sexual object, which would normally be rapidly passed through on the way towards the final sexual goal.

A) Anatomical Transgressions

(OVER-VALUATION OF THE SEXUAL OBJECT)

The psychical esteem in which the sexual object is held as an ideal goal for the sexual drive is limited to the genitals only in the rarest cases, instead extending to the body as a whole, and tends to involve all the sensations emanating from the sexual object. The same over-valuation spreads into the psychical field, where it appears as a blinding of logic (weakness of judgement) concerning the sexual object's mental accomplishments and perfections, as well as a credulous submissiveness to the latter's judgements. The credulity of love thus becomes an important, if not the primary, source of authority.

It is this sexual over-valuation that sits so ill with the restriction of the sexual goal to the union of the actual genitals, and contributes to the turning of other body parts into sexual goals.

The significance of the element of sexual over-valuation can be most easily studied in men, whose love-life is the only one to have become amenable to examination, while that of women is still shrouded in impenetrable obscurity as a result both of cultural atrophy and of women's secrecy and insincerity.

(SEXUAL USE OF THE MUCOUS MEMBRANE OF THE LIPS AND MOUTH)

The use of the mouth as a sexual organ is considered to be a perversion when the lips (or tongue) of one person are brought into contact with the genitals of the other, but not if the mucous membranes of the lips of both parties touch one another. The latter exception establishes contact with normality. Anyone who abhors the other practices, which have been customary since the earliest times of humanity, will yield to a distinct *feeling of disgust*, which protects him against the acceptance of such a sexual goal. The limit of this disgust, however, is often purely conventional; someone who ardently kisses the lips of a beautiful girl might not be able to use her toothbrush without a feeling of disgust, although there is no reason to assume that his own oral cavity, which does not disgust him, is any cleaner than the girl's. Our attention is drawn here to the element of disgust, which gets in the way of the libidinal overvaluation of the sexual object, but which can in turn be overcome by the libido. One would be inclined to see disgust as one of the powers which have imposed boundaries upon the sexual goal. As a rule, these stop short of the genitals themselves. But there is no doubt that the genitals of the opposite sex can in themselves be an object of disgust, and that this attitude is one of the characteristics of all hysterics (particularly among females). The strength of the sexual drive enjoys actively overcoming this disgust. (See below.)

(SEXUAL USE OF THE ANAL ORIFICE)

Where the utilization of the anus is concerned, it is easier to see that it is disgust that stamps this sexual goal as a perversion than in the case mentioned above. But I do not wish it to be considered as bias on my part if I observe that the explanation for this disgust, the fact that this body part fulfils the purpose of excretion and comes into contact with something inherently disgusting – excrement – does not have much more validity than the explanation given by hysterical girls for their disgust in the face of male genitals: they serve to evacuate urine.

The sexual role of the anal mucous membrane is by no means restricted to intercourse between men, and there is nothing about it to make it characteristic of inverted feeling. On the contrary, it appears that pederasty among men owes its role to analogy with the act with a woman, while mutual masturbation is the most usual sexual goal in intercourse between inverts.

(SIGNIFICANCE OF OTHER BODY PARTS)

There is in principle nothing new about the sexual encroachment upon other parts of the body, in all its variations, and it adds nothing to our knowledge of the sexual drive, which is merely announcing its intention to go in every possible direction to take power of the sexual object. Sexual over-valuation aside, however, in anatomical transgressions a second element alien to popular knowledge becomes apparent. Certain parts of the body, such as the mucous membrance of the mouth and the anus, which repeatedly appear in these practices, effectively lay claim to be considered and treated as genitals in their own right. We will hear how this claim is justified by the development of the sexual drive, and how it is fulfilled in the symptomatology of certain illnesses.

(INAPPROPRIATE REPLACEMENT OF THE SEXUAL OBJECT — FETISHISM)

A quite particular impression is created by those cases in which the normal sexual object is replaced by another which is connected to it, but which is utterly unsuited to the accomplishment of the normal sexual goal. From the point of view of categorization we should perhaps have mentioned this extremely interesting group of deviations related to the sexual drive among the deviations related to the sexual object, but we have put off doing so until we have encountered the element of *sexual over-valuation* on which these phenomena depend, and which is connected with an abandonment of the sexual goal.

The substitute for the sexual object is a body part (foot, hair) which is generally unsuited to sexual purposes, or an inanimate object demonstrably connected to the sexual person, or best of all with that person's sexuality (items of clothing, white linen). It is not without some justification that this substitution is compared with the fetish in which primitive man sees his god embodied.

The transition to those cases of fetishism in which a normal or perverse sexual goal is abandoned occurs in cases where a fetishistic condition is required of the sexual object if the sexual goal is to be accomplished (a particular hair colour, clothing, even physical imperfections). No other variation of the sexual drive verging on the pathological is of such great interest to us as this one, because of the strangeness of the phenomena to which it gives rise. A certain reduction in striving for the normal sexual goal seems to be the precondition for all such cases (executive weakness of the sexual apparatus). The link to normality is conveyed by the psychologically necessary over-valuation of the sexual object, which inevitably encroaches upon everything connected with it by association. Hence a certain degree of such fetishism is a regular part of normal loving, particularly during those stages when one is in love, in which the normal sexual goal appears unattainable or its fulfilment cancelled.

> *Schaff' mir ein Halstuch von ihrer Brust,*
> *Ein Strumpfband meiner Liebeslust!*
>
> [Bring me a kerchief from her breast,
>   A garter of my love's delight!]
>   (Faust)

The pathological case only occurs when the striving for the fetish becomes fixated beyond such conditions and takes the place of the normal goal, or if the fetish breaks free of the particular person and itself becomes the sole sexual object. These are the general conditions for the transition from mere variations in the sexual drive to pathological aberrations.

In the choice of the fetish, as Alfred Binet first claimed – and this has subsequently been proven with ample evidence – what is revealed is the continuing influence of a sexual impression generally received in early childhood, and which we may place next to the proverbial retentiveness of first love in a normal person (*'on revient toujours à ses premiers amours'* ['we always return to our first loves']). Such a deduction is particularly clear in cases in which the sexual object is merely fetishistically conditioned. We shall encounter the importance of early sexual impressions elsewhere.

In other cases it is a symbolic connection of ideas, of which the person affected is not generally conscious, that has led to the replacement of the object by the fetish. The routes of these connections are not always demonstrable with any great certainty (the foot is an ancient sexual symbol, even in myth, and fur probably owes its fetishistic role to its association with the hair covering the mons veneris); but such symbolism does not always appear to be independent of childhood sexual experiences.

B) Fixations of Temporary Sexual Goals

(APPEARANCE OF NEW INTENTIONS)

All those external and internal conditions which obstruct or defer the accomplishment of the normal sexual goal (impotence, the high cost of the sexual object, dangers of the sexual act) understandably support the inclination to linger over the preparatory acts and turn them into new sexual goals which can replace the normal goals. On closer examination it always proves that those new intentions which appear most alien are already hinted at in normal sexual processes.

(TOUCHING AND LOOKING)

A certain degree of touching is, at least for human beings, indispensable for the achievement of the normal sexual goal. It is also a matter of general knowledge that the touch of the sexual object's skin constitutes on the one hand a great source of pleasure and on the other a great influx of arousal. Consequently, lingering over the touch, if the sexual act then continues further, can hardly be counted among the perversions.

Much the same is true of seeing, which is ultimately derived from touching. The optical impression remains the path along which libidinous arousal is most frequently awoken, and on whose viability – if this teleological way of looking at things may be permitted – breeding selection depends, in that it allows the sexual object to develop into something beautiful. The uncovering of the body, which is advancing along with civilization, keeps alive the sexual curiosity which seeks to complete the sexual object by revealing its hidden parts, but which can be diverted ('sublimated') into art if its interest can be distracted from the genitals to the form of the body as a whole. Lingering over this intermediate sexual goal of sexually emphasized look-ing appears among most normal people, indeed it gives them the opportunity to elevate a certain proportion of their libido to higher artistic goals. The love of looking becomes a perversion, on the other hand, a) if it is restricted exclusively to the genitals, b) if it is linked to the overcoming of disgust (voyeurs: those who watch the functions of excretion), or c) if it represses the normal sexual goal rather than preparing for it. The latter is true to a most pronounced degree among exhi-bitionists who, if I may draw this conclusion on the basis of several analyses, show their genitals in order to see the genitals of the other party in return.

In the perversion whose efforts are concerned with looking and being looked at, a very curious character-istic emerges, which will preoccupy us even more intensely in the next deviation. The sexual goal is present in two formations, the active and the passive.

The power which stands in the way of the love of looking, and which may be cancelled by it, is *shame* (as disgust was before).

(SADISM AND MASOCHISM)

The inclination to cause pain to the sexual object, and its counterpart, this most frequent and significant of all perversions, has been identified by Krafft-Ebing, in its two formations, the active and the passive, as *sadism* and *masochism*. Other authors prefer the narrower term *algolagnia*, which stresses the pleasure in pain and cruelty, while the names chosen by Krafft-Ebing stress the pleasure to be had from all kinds of humiliation and subjection.

Where active algolagnia, sadism, is concerned, its roots in the normal person can be easily demonstrated. Most men's sexuality reveals a certain quantity of *aggression*, of the inclination to overpower, whose biological significance lies perhaps in the need to overcome the resistance of the sexual object in a way other than the acts involved in *courtship*. In that case, sadism might be thought to correspond to an aggressive component of the sexual drive which has now become autonomous and exaggerated by virtue of being shifted into the leading position.

The concept of sadism varies in linguistic usage from a merely active, and violent, attitude towards the sexual object, to the exclusive derivation of satisfaction from the object's subjection and mistreatment. Strictly speaking, only the latter, extreme case may properly be deemed a perversion.

Similarly, the term masochism encompasses all passive attitudes towards sexual life and the sexual object, the most extreme form of which derives its satisfaction from the suffering of physical or mental pain inflicted by the sexual object. As a perversion, masochism seems further removed from the normal sexual goal than its positive counterpart; we may doubt whether it is ever a primary phenomenon, or whether it does not universally emerge as a transformation of sadism. It is often apparent that masochism is nothing but an extension of sadism turned upon the subject's own person, which thereby comes to occupy the position of the sexual object. Clinical analysis of extreme cases of masochistic perversion suggests the combination of many elements working together to exaggerate and fixate the original passive sexual attitude (castration complex, sense of guilt).

The pain thus overcome joins the disgust and shame that had acted as resistances to the libido.

Sadism and masochism assume a particular place among the perversions, since their underlying opposition of activity and passivity is among the universal characteristics of sexual life.

The cultural history of mankind teaches us beyond any doubt that cruelty and the sexual urge belong most profoundly together, but in making this connection clear we have not gone beyond an emphasis on the aggressive element of the libido. According to some commentators, the combination of this aggression with the sexual drive is actually a leftover from cannibalistic pleasures, associated with the apparatus involved in overpowering, which serves to satisfy the other, onto-genetically older, major need. It has also been asserted that every pain contains within itself the possibility of a feeling of pleasure. We shall merely observe that this perversion has not been satisfactorily explained, and that it may be the case that several different mental efforts combine within it to create a single effect.

The most striking quality of this perversion, however, lies in the fact that its active and passive forms are regularly encountered in one and the same person. Anyone who takes pleasure in causing others pain in a sexual relationship is also capable of enjoying as pleasure the pain that can arise from his own sexual relations. A sadist is always at the same time a masochist, although the active or the passive side of the perversion may be more strongly developed in him, and either one can represent his predominant sexual activity.

Thus we can see that certain inclinations towards perversion regularly appear as *pairs of opposites*; in relation to material which will be introduced below, this may claim a high level of theoretical significance. It is also illuminating that the existence of the pair of opposites, sadism and masochism, cannot simply be deduced by the presence of aggression. On the other hand, one might be tempted to connect such simultaneously existing opposites with the opposites of male and female united in bisexuality, for which active and passive can often be used in psychoanalysis.

3) General Observations Concerning all Perversions

(VARIATION AND ILLNESS)

Doctors who have first studied the perversions in highly pronounced examples and under particular conditions have naturally been inclined to attribute to them the characteristics of illness or degeneracy, just as they have with inversion. In the latter case it is easier to reject this view. Everyday experience has shown that most of these transgressions, at least the less serious among them, form a component that is rarely absent from the sexual life of healthy people, and are also held by them to resemble other intimacies. Conditions permitting, even a normal person can replace the normal sexual goal with such a perversion for some considerable time, or allow the two to coincide. In every healthy person a supplement that might be called perverse is present in the normal sexual goal, and this universality is sufficient in itself to suggest the pointlessness of using the term 'perversion' in an accusatory sense. It is precisely in the area of sexual life that we encounter particular and currently insoluble difficulties if we wish to draw a sharp distinction between mere variation within the physiological range and pathological symptoms.

In some of these perversions the quality of the new sexual goal is such that it requires particular appreciation. Certain perversions are, in terms of their content, so far removed from normality that we cannot help but declare them 'pathological', particularly those in which the sexual drive performs astonishing feats (licking excrement, abusing corpses) in overcoming resistances (shame, disgust, fear, pain). But even in cases such as these we should not allow ourselves to expect with any certainty that the perpetrators will inevitably turn out to be people with different serious abnormalities, or people who are mentally ill. Here, too, we cannot escape the fact that individuals who behave normally in other respects reveal themselves in the area of sexual life alone, under the domination of the most unbridled of all the drives, to be ill. Manifest abnormality in other relations of life, on the other hand, always tends to show a background of abnormal sexual behaviour.

In the majority of cases we can find a pathological

character in the perversion, not in the content of the new sexual goal, but in its relation to the normal. It is where the perversion does not appear *alongside* the normal (sexual goal and object), where favourable conditions encourage the perversion and unfavourable circumstances obstruct the normal, but has repressed and replaced the normal under all circumstances; it is in the *exclusiveness* and *fixation* of the perversion that we are most generally justified in diagnosing it as a pathological symptom.

(MENTAL PARTICIPATION IN THE PERVERSIONS)

It is perhaps in the case of the most repellent perversions that we must acknowledge the most generous psychical participation in the transformation of the sexual drive. Here a mental task is being performed which, despite its grim consequences, we are obliged to see as an idealization of the drive. It may be that the omnipotence of love is nowhere more strongly apparent than in these deviations. Everywhere in sexuality, the highest and the lowest are most profoundly attached to one another ('from heaven through the world to hell' [*Faust*]).

(TWO RESULTS)

In the course of our study of perversions we have come to understand that the sexual drive has to struggle against certain mental forces which act as resistances, shame and disgust appearing most clearly among them. We may suppose that these forces are involved in keeping the drive within what may be seen as normal bounds, and if they have developed in the individual before the sexual drive has reached its full strength, it was probably they that suggested the direction of its development.

We have also observed that some of the perversions investigated can only be understood where a number of motives coincide. If they permit analysis – or dissection – they must be composite in nature. We may take this as a sign that the sexual drive itself is perhaps not something simple, but is rather assembled out of components that come apart again in the perversions. If this is so, clinical observation has brought our attention to *fusions* that have lost their manifestation in uniform normal behaviour.

4) The Sexual Drive in Neurotics

(PSYCHOANALYSIS)

One important contribution to our knowledge of the sexual drive in people who are at least close to normality is derived from a source that is only accessible in one particular way. There is only one means of forming thorough and reliable conclusions about the sexual life of so-called psychoneurotics (hysteria, compulsive neurosis, wrongly called neurasthenia, certainly also dementia praecox, paranoia), and that is by subjecting them to psychoanalytical investigation, using the healing process employed by J. Breuer and myself in 1893, which we then called 'cathartic'.

I should first explain, or rather repeat from other publications, that these psychoneuroses, as far as my experiences extend, are based on sexual drive-forces. I do not mean to say by this that the energy of the sexual drive contributes to the forces that maintain the pathological manifestations (the symptoms), but I wish expressly to stress that this contribution is the only constant energy source for neurosis, and the most important one. Consequently, the sexual life of the people in question is expressed exclusively, predominantly or only partially in these symptoms. The symptoms are, as I have said elsewhere, the patient's sexual activity. My proof for this claim has lain in a growing number of psychoanalyses of hysterics and others suffering from nervous disorders. I have given a detailed account of the results of these elsewhere and shall continue to do so.

Psychoanalysis removes the symptoms of hysterics on the basis that they are substitutes – transcriptions, we might say – for a series of affect-laden mental processes, desires and strivings which, as the result of a particular psychical process (*repression*), have been denied the possibility of fulfilment in psychical activity that is capable of reaching consciousness. Hence these thought-formations, retained in a state of unconsciousness, strive for an expression appropriate to their affective value, a *discharge*, and find this in hysteria through the process of *conversion* to somatic phenomena – the hysterical symptoms. If a particular technique is skilfully employed to transform the symptoms back into conscious, emotionally invested ideas, we are in a position to learn something very precise about the nature and ancestry of these previously unconscious psychical formations.

(RESULTS OF PSYCHOANALYSIS)

Thus we have learned that symptoms are substitutes for strivings which draw their power from the source of the sexual drive. This fully accords with what we know of the character of hysterics – taken here as a model for all psychoneurotics – before they fall ill, and with what we know of the causes of their illness. The hysterical character exhibits a degree of *sexual repression* beyond that which we may consider normal, an intensification of those resistances to the sexual drive known to us as shame, disgust and morality, and an almost instinctive flight from intellectual preoccupation with the problem of sex, which in pronounced cases successfully preserves complete sexual ignorance into the age of sexual maturity.

In many cases this character trait, essential to hysteria, is concealed from the untrained observer by the presence of the second constitutional factor involved in hysteria: the overwhelming formation of the sexual drive. Only psychological analysis can reveal this in every case, and solve the mystery of hysteria, with all its inconsistencies, by establishing the pair of opposites consisting of an excessive sexual need and an exaggerated aversion to sex.

The occasion for illness arises in the person with a predisposition to hysteria when, because of that person's own developing maturity or the external conditions of their life, they face real and serious sexual demands. Between the compulsions of the drive and the resistance of sexual refusal, the person then finds the solution of illness. It does not resolve the conflict, but seeks to elude it by transforming libidinal strivings into symptoms. It is only apparently exceptional if a hysterical person, a man, for example, falls ill under the influence of a banal emotion, a conflict without sexual interest at its centre. In all cases, psychoanalysis is then able to demonstrate that it is the sexual component of the conflict that has made the illness possible by removing the mental processes from their normal execution.

(NEUROSIS AND PERVERSION)

Many objections to these findings are probably explained by the fact that sexuality, from which I deduce the psychoneurotic symptoms, is equated with the normal sexual drive. But psychoanalysis goes further than that. It shows that symptoms do not arise only at the expense of the so-called normal sexual drive (at least not exclusively or predominantly), but represent the converted expression of drives which would be described as *perverse* (in the broadest sense) if they could be expressed in fantasy intentions and actions undistracted by consciousness. The symptoms are thus formed partly at the expense of abnormal sexuality; *neurosis is, we might say, the negative of perversion.*

The sexual drive of psychoneurotics exhibits all the deviations that we have studied as variations of the normal, and expressions of the pathological, sexual life. a) In the unconscious mental life of all neurotics (without exception) we will find impulses of inversion, and the fixation of the libido on people of the same sex. The significance of this factor for an understanding of the illness cannot be properly assessed without deeper discussion. I can only assure the reader that the unconscious tendency towards inversion is never absent, and in particular that it provides great help in explaining male hysteria.

b) Among psychoneurotics, all tendencies to anatomical transgressions are demonstrably present in the unconscious and in the formation of symptoms. Particularly frequent and intense among them are those that assign the role of the genitals to the mucous membrane of the mouth and the anus.

c) The partial drives play quite a prominent role in forming the symptoms of psychoneuroses. Mostly apparent in pairs of opposites, we have encountered them introducing new sexual goals, the drive to the love of looking and exhibitionism, and the drive to cruelty in both active and passive formations. The contribution of the latter is indispensable for an understanding of the presence of *suffering* in the symptoms, and in almost every case it controls part of the patient's social behaviour. Through this link between cruelty and the libido, love is also transformed into hatred, and tender impulses into hostile ones. This is entirely characteristic of a whole series of neurotic cases, indeed, it would appear, of paranoia in general.

Interest in these results is only heightened by certain special facts.

α) Where a drive of this kind is discovered in the unconscious, and is capable of pairing with an opposite, in almost every case the opposite can be shown to take effect as well. Each 'active' perversion is thus accompanied here by its passive counterpart: someone who is unconsciously an exhibitionist is also and at the same time a voyeur, and in anyone suffering the consequences of the repression of sadistic impulses we will encounter an additional influx of symptoms drawing on the sources of the tendency towards masochism. The complete agreement with what we have discovered about the corresponding 'positive' perversions is most worthy of note. In our understanding of the illness, however, one or the other of the opposing inclinations plays the predominant role.

β) In a more pronounced case of psychoneurosis we only rarely encounter one of these perverse drives on its own. More generally we find a larger number of these and usually traces of all of them; however, the individual drive is, in its intensity, independent of the formation of the others. Here, too, the study of positive perversions provides us with a precise counterpart.

5) Partial Drives and Erogenous Zones

Considering all that we have learned from our investigation of the positive and negative perversions, it seems reasonable to trace these back to a series of 'partial drives'. These are not primary, but they do permit further interpretation. At first the word 'drive' suggests nothing but the psychical representation of a continuously flowing, internal somatic source of stimuli, in contrast to 'stimulus', which is produced by individual external excitements. 'Drive' is thus one of the terms that separate the mental from the physical. The simplest and most obvious assumption about the nature of drives would be that they have no inherent quality of their own, and only come into consideration in so far as they give work to the mental life. What distinguishes the drives from one another and gives them specific qualities is their relationship to their somatic *sources* and their *goals*. The source of the drive is a process of excitement in an organ, and the immediate goal of the drive lies in the removal of that organic stimulus.

A further provisional assumption in drive theory, and one which we are unable to escape, tells us that the physical organs provide two kinds of excitement, based in differences that are chemical in nature. One of these kinds of excitement we describe as specifically sexual, and the organ in question as the *'erogenous zone'* of the partial drive that issues from it.

In the perverse tendencies which place a sexual significance upon the oral cavity and the anal orifice, the role of the erogenous zone is immediately clear. In all respects it behaves like a piece of the sexual apparatus. In hysteria, these body parts and their tracts of mucous membrane similarly become the site of new sensations and changes in innervation – indeed of processes that can be compared to penile erection – just as the genitals themselves do in response to the stimuli of normal sexual processes.

The significance of the erogenous zones as secondary apparatuses and surrogates for the genitals becomes most clearly apparent in the case of psychoneuroses, although this is not to claim that it is any less important for other kinds of illness. It is only less discernible here because in these illnesses (compulsive neurosis, paranoia) the symptoms are formed in regions of the mental apparatus which lie further from the individual centres responsible for physical control. In compulsive neurosis, the significance of the impulses that create new sexual goals, and which appear independent of erogenous zones, is the more striking. But with the love of looking and exhibitionism the eye corresponds to an erogenous zone, in the case of the pain and cruelty component of the sexual drive it is the skin that assumes the same role, having at particular points in the body become differentiated into sensual organs and modified into mucous membranes: the erogenous zone κατ' 'εξοχήν [*par excellence*].

6) Explanation of the Apparent Predominance of Perverse Sexuality in Psychoneuroses

As a result of the above discussions, the sexuality of psychoneurotics may have been shown in a false light. It has come to appear as though psychoneurotics were brought, by their predisposition, very close to perversion in their sexual behaviour, and conversely removed equally far from normality. Now it may very well be that the constitutional predisposition of these patients, aside from an excessive degree of sexual repression and an overwhelmingly strong sexual drive, contains among other things an unusual tendency towards perversion in the broadest sense. However, the examination of less severe cases shows that we need not necessarily make this assumption, or at least that in our assessment of the pathological effects there is another factor moving in the opposite direction. Among most psychoneurotics, the illness only appears after puberty in the face of the requirements of normal sexual life. It is particularly at the latter that repression is directed. Or else later illnesses are generated when the libido cannot be satisfied in the normal way. In both cases the libido behaves like a stream the main bed of which is moved to a different place; it fills the collateral paths that might previously have been empty. In this way the inclination towards perversion among psychoneurotics, apparently so great (although negative), may also be collaterally conditioned, but must be collaterally intensified. The fact is that sexual repression as an internal element must be categorized along with those external elements such as restrictions on freedom, lack of access to the normal sexual object, dangers involved in the normal sexual act and so on, which create perversions in individuals who might otherwise have remained normal.

The situation may differ between different individual cases of neurosis: in one, the innate level of the inclination towards perversion may be made important, and in another its collateral intensification by the diversion of the libido from the normal sexual goal and sexual object. It would be unfair to construct an opposition in which a relationship of co-operation actually prevails. The greatest accomplishments of neurosis will always occur when constitution and experience co-operate in the same direction. A marked constitution, for example, will be able to manage without support from the impressions of life, while a substantial shock in life might bring the neurosis into being even in the case of an average constitution. These views, incidentally, apply equally to the aetiological significance of the innate and to accidental experience in other areas.

If one prefers to assume that a particularly well-developed tendency towards perversions is one of the peculiarities of the psychoneurotic constitution, one has a greater chance, depending on the innate preponderance of one erogenous zone or another, of differentiating between a great variety of such constitutions in one or other of the partial drives. The question of whether the perverse predisposition has a particular relationship to the choice of the form of illness has, like so much else in this field, not yet been investigated.

7) Reference to the Infantilism of Sexuality

By demonstrating the part played by perverse impulses in the formation of symptoms in psychoneuroses, we have increased the number of people who would count as perverts to a quite extraordinary level. Not only do neurotics themselves represent a very numerous class of people: it should also be borne in mind that all forms of neurosis shade off in uninterrupted series to health; Moebius was, after all, justified in saying: we are all a little hysterical. Consequently we are forced by the extraordinary distribution of perversions to assume that even the predisposition towards perversions must not be something rare and special but is part of the constitution that is considered normal.

We have heard that there is some contention about whether the perversions derive from innate conditions or arise as a result of chance experiences, as Binet assumed in the case of fetishism. Now we are presented with the decision that there is something innate underlying perversions, but that it is something *innate in everyone*, since a predisposition may vary in intensity, and waits to be brought to the fore by the influences of life. What is at issue are the innate roots of the sexual drive, which in many cases develop into the true vehicles of sexual activity (perversions), and in others are insufficiently suppressed (repression) so that they are indirectly able to draw to themselves a considerable share of sexual energy as symptoms of illness, while in the most favourable cases which fall between these two extremes, they bring about a so-called normal sex life by means of effective restriction and other forms of modification.

But we shall also note that the hypothetical constitution, containing the seeds of all perversions, will only be apparent in children, even if all drives appear only at modest intensities in the child. If we are becoming aware of the formula that the sexuality of neurotics has remained in an infantile state, or else has been returned to that state, our interest will turn towards the sexual lives of children, and we will want to pursue the interplay of those influences that dominate the developmental process of child sexuality to its outcome in perversion, neurosis or a normal sex life.

The Virginity Taboo

Few details of the sexual life of primitive peoples have such a surprising effect on our emotions as their assessment of virginity, the intact state of the woman. To us, the high regard placed upon virginity by the suitor is so solidly established and self-evident that we almost become embarrassed if called upon to explain it. The requirement that the girl should not bring into marriage to one husband a memory of sexual intercourse with another is of course nothing but the consistent continuation of the exclusive property right to a woman which constitutes the essence of monogamy, and the extension of this monopoly to include the past.

So it is not difficult for us to justify what at first seemed to us to be a prejudice, on the basis of our opinions about a woman's erotic life. The person who is first able to satisfy the virgin's longing for love, arduously contained over a long period of time, and who has thus overcome the resistances erected in her by the influences of milieu and her education, will be drawn by her into a lasting relationship that will no longer be possible with anyone else. On the basis of this experience the woman enters a state of dependence which guarantees the untroubled permanence of her possession and makes her capable of resisting new impressions and the temptations of strangers.

The expression 'sexual bondage' was chosen in 1892 by Krafft-Ebing to describe the fact that individuals can acquire an unusually high degree of bondage with, and a lack of autonomy towards, another person with whom they are having sexual intercourse. This bondage can sometimes extend very far, as far as the loss of all autonomous will and the toleration of the most severe sacrifices of the person's own interests; the author, however, has not neglected to observe that a certain degree of such bondage is 'entirely necessary if the connection is to be of some duration'. Such a degree of sexual bondage is in fact indispensable to the maintenance of the civilized marriage and the curbing of the polygamous tendencies that threaten it, and in our social community this factor is regularly taken into account.

An 'unusual degree of passionate love and weakness of character' on the one hand, boundless egoism on the other: Krafft-Ebing deduces the origin of sexual bondage from the coincidence of these two factors. Analytic experiences, however, mean that we cannot content ourselves with this simple attempt at an explanation. Rather, it becomes apparent that the crucial factor is the amount of sexual resistance that is overcome, along with the concentration and uniqueness of the process of overcoming it. Accordingly, bondage is incomparably more frequent and intense in women than in men, although in our own times it is more frequent in men than it was in antiquity. Where we have been able to study sexual dependence in men, it has been shown to be the result of the overcoming of a psychical impotence by a particular woman, to whom the man in question has felt bound from that point onwards. This course of events seems to explain many unusual marriages and some tragic fates, even some of far-reaching importance.

We would not be properly describing the behaviour of primitive peoples if we said that they placed no emphasis on virginity, adducing as proof that they allow the defloration of girls outside of wedlock and before the first act of marital intercourse. It appears on the contrary that for these people, too, defloration is a significant act, but it has become the object of a taboo, a prohibition that could be called religious. Instead of making the accomplishment of the act the preserve of the girl's fiancé and later husband, custom requires that *he should avoid it*.

It is not my intention to make a complete collection of all the literary testimonies for the existence of this moral prohibition, to pursue its geographic spread and list all the forms in which it is expressed. So I shall merely state that it is very widespread practice among primitive peoples living today to remove the hymen in this way, outside the marriage that will subsequently take place. Crawley puts it as follows: 'This marriage ceremony consists in perforation of the hymen by some appointed person other than the husband; it is common in the lowest stages of culture, especially in Australia.'

But if defloration is not to occur as a result of the first act of marital intercourse, it must be undertaken – somehow, by someone – before this. I shall cite some passages from Crawley's book mentioned above, which are informative on these points, but which also justify us in making our own critical observations.

p. 191: 'Thus in the Dieri and neighbouring tribes (in Australia) it is the universal custom when a girl reaches puberty to rupture the hymen (*Journ. Anthrop. Inst.*, XXIV, 169). In the Portland and Glenelg tribes this is done to the bride by an old woman; and sometimes white men are asked for this reason to deflower maidens (Brough Smith, op. cit., II, 319).'

p. 307: 'The artificial rupture of the hymen sometimes takes place in infancy, but generally at puberty . . . It is often combined, as in Australia, with a ceremonial act of intercourse.'

p. 348: (On Australian tribes where the well-known exogamous restrictions on marriage prevail, from communications by Spencer and Gillen): 'The hymen is artificially perforated, and then the assisting men have access (ceremonial, be it observed) to the girl in a stated order . . . The act is in two parts, perforation and intercourse.'

p. 349. 'An important preliminary of marriage amongst the Masai (in Equatorial Africa) is the performance of this operation on the girl (J. Thompson, op. cit., 258). This defloration is performed by the father of the bride among the Sakais (Malay), Battas (Sumatra) and Alfoers of Celebes (Ploss and Bartels, op. cit., II, 490). In the Philippines there were certain men whose profession it was to deflower brides, in case the hymen had not been ruptured in childhood by an old woman who was sometimes employed for this (Featherman, op. cit., II, 474). The defloration of the bride was amongst some Eskimo tribes entrusted to the angekok, or priest (ibid., III, 406).'

The observations that I have reported refer to two points. First, it is regrettable that in these accounts no more careful distinction has been made between the rupture of the hymen without coitus and coitus for the purpose of such a rupture. Only at one point do we expressly hear that the process is divided into two parts, the (manual or instrumental) defloration and the subsequent sex act. The otherwise very rich material in Bartels and Ploss is almost unusable for our purposes because in this account the psychological significance of the act of defloration, as against its anatomical result, is completely absent. Secondly, one would like to be told in what respect 'ceremonial' (purely formal, solemn, official) coitus on these occasions differs from regular sexual intercourse. The authors to whom I have had access were either too ashamed to say anything about it, or underestimated the psychological significance of such sexual details. We may hope that the original reports of travellers and missionaries are more thorough and unambiguous, but given the current difficulty of getting access to this generally foreign literature I can say nothing definite about it. Besides, we may dispel any doubts concerning this second point by observing that ceremonial, mock coitus represents only a substitute, perhaps a replacement, for an act that was performed in its entirety in former times.

To explain this virginity taboo, various different elements might be introduced, of which I shall give a brief account. The defloration of girls generally involves the spilling of blood; the first attempt at explanation then refers to primitive man's fear of blood, with blood being seen as the seat of life. This blood taboo has been proven by numerous proscriptions that have nothing to do with sexuality. It clearly has something to do with the prohibition on killing and forms a protective defence against the primal thirst for blood, primeval man's lust for killing. In this view, the taboo of virginity is allied with the almost universal taboo on menstruation. Primitive man cannot separate the mysterious phenomenon of the monthly blood flow from sadistic ideas. He interprets menstruation, particularly the first time it occurs, as the bite of a spirit animal, perhaps as the sign of sexual intercourse with that spirit. According to some, he recognizes this spirit as that of an ancestor, and then we understand, borrowing on other insights, that the menstruating girl is taboo because she is a property of this ancestral spirit.

On the other hand, however, we are warned not to overestimate the influence of a factor such as a horror of blood. After all, no such horror has succeeded in suppressing practices such as the circumcision of boys and the even crueller circumcision of girls (excision of the clitoris and the labia minor), which are practised to some extent among the same people, or in abolishing the validity of other ceremonies during which blood is spilt. So it could hardly come as a surprise if that fear had been overcome to the benefit of the husband on the occasion of the first cohabitation.

A second explanation also turns away from the

sexual, but reaches much further into the universal. It suggests that primitive man is the prey to a persistent anxious disposition that constantly lies in wait, very like the one that we assert in the psychoanalytic theory of neuroses. This anxious disposition is most apparent on all occasions which depart in some way from the familiar, and which introduce something new and unexpected, something not understood or strange and sinister. This is also the source of the ceremonial that extends far into later religions, and which is connected to the start of any new task, to the beginning of any new period of time, to first fruits, whether they be human, animal or vegetable. The dangers by which the anxious person believes himself threatened never present themselves more vividly to him than on the threshold of the dangerous situation, and it is then only sensible to protect oneself against them. The first act of sexual intercourse can certainly claim, because of its importance, to be preceded by such cautionary measures. The two attempts at explanation, based on the fear of blood and the fear of first occasions, do not contradict, but rather reinforce one another. The first act of sexual intercourse in marriage is certainly a serious act, all the more so if it is to involve the flow of blood.

A third explanation – the one preferred by Crawley – points out that the virginity taboo belongs in a wider context, encompassing the whole of the sexual life. It is not only the first coitus with the woman that is taboo, but sexual intercourse in general; we might almost say that woman as a whole is taboo. Woman is not only taboo in particular situations deriving from her sexual life – menstruation, pregnancy, childbirth and confinement. Even outside of these situations, intercourse with a woman is subject to prohibitions so serious and so numerous that we have every reason to doubt the supposed sexual freedom of primitive people. It is correct that the sexuality of primitive peoples is on certain occasions free of inhibitions; usually, however, it seems to be more strongly bound by prohibitions than it is at higher levels of civilization. Whenever men undertake something special, an expedition, a hunt, a war campaign, they must stay far from women, particularly from sexual intercourse with them; otherwise it will paralyse their strength and bring failure. Even in the customs of daily life, efforts to keep the sexes apart are unmistakable. Women live with women, men with men; family life in our sense is thought barely to exist in many primitive tribes. The separation is sometimes taken so far that one sex is forbidden to pronounce the personal names of the other sex, and women develop a language with a special vocabulary. Sexual need may repeatedly break through these barriers of separation, but in some tribes even meetings between the spouses must take place outside the house and in secret.

Wherever primitive man has set a taboo, he fears a danger, and we should not dismiss the idea that all these prescriptions of avoidance manifest an essential fear of woman. Perhaps this fear is based on the fact that women appear different from men, eternally incomprehensible and mysterious, strange and therefore hostile. Men fear that women will weaken them, infecting them with their femininity, and that the men will consequently prove to be unfit. The sleep-inducing, relaxing effect of coitus may be the model for this fear, and along with the perception of the influence that women acquire through sexual inter-course with men, and the consideration that they com-pel, may justify the spread of that fear. There is nothing ancient about all this, nothing that does not live on among us.

Many observers of primitive people living today have judged that their tendencies towards love are relatively weak, and never reach the intensity that we are used to finding among civilized people. Others have contra-dicted this assessment, but at any rate the taboo prac-tices listed above reveal a power that contradicts love in rejecting the woman as strange and hostile.

In terms little different from the usual terminology of psychoanalysis, Crawley reveals that each individual is separated from the others through a 'taboo of per-sonal isolation', and that it is precisely the small differ-ences, all else being similar, that explain the feelings of strangeness and hostility between them. It would be tempting to pursue this idea and deduce from this 'narcissism of small differences' the hostility that we see successfully arguing against the feelings of solidarity and the commandment of universal human love. As to the basis for the narcissistic, highly contemptuous rejection of women by men, psychoanalysis believes it has guessed a chief cause in the castration complex and its influence on the judgement of women.

However, we note that these last observations have

taken us far beyond our theme. The universal taboo on women sheds no light on the particular prescriptions set down for the first sexual act with the individual virgin. Here we are referred back to our initial explanations: the fear of blood and the fear of the first occasion, and even of these we would have to say that they do not get to the heart of the taboo precept. This is quite clearly based on the intention of *refusing or sparing the later husband* something inseparable from the first sexual act, although, according to the observation we made at the beginning, this relationship would require a particular bond between the woman and that particular man.

This is not the place to discuss the origin and the ultimate significance of the taboo prescriptions. I have done that in my book *Totem and Taboo*, where I acknowledged the condition of an original ambivalence for the taboo and argued that its origins lay in prehistoric processes that have led to the foundation of the human family. We can no longer discern such a primal significance in the taboo customs practised by primitives today. We forget all too easily that even the most primitive peoples live in a culture far removed from the primeval, one which is, in chronological terms, just as old as our own and which similarly corresponds to a later, albeit different, stage of development.

Today we find that taboos among primitives have already been spun into a deft system, much like the ones developed by our own neurotics in their phobias, in which ancient motives are replaced with more recent ones which harmoniously agree. Setting aside these genetic problems, then, we wish to return to the insight that primitive man applies a taboo where he fears a danger. This danger is, it is generally understood, a psychical one, because the primitive is not obliged to make two distinctions that strike us as unavoidable. He does not separate the material danger from the psychical, or the real from the imaginary. In his consistent animistic view of the world, all danger – both the danger that comes from a natural force and that from other people or animals – arises from the hostile intention of a creature which possesses a soul just as he does. On the other hand, however, he is accustomed to projecting his own inner impulses of hostility on to the outside world, and shifting them on to the objects which he feels to be unpleasant or even merely strange. Women are also now recognized as a source of such dangers, and the first sexual act with a woman is marked out as a particularly intense danger.

I believe that we will obtain some information about the nature of this intensified danger, and why it particularly threatens the future husband, if we examine the behaviour of contemporary women at our own stage of civilization more precisely in the same context. I can confirm as a result of this examination that such a danger really does exist, and this proves that with the virginity taboo, primitive man is defending himself against a danger that he is right to suspect, although it is a psychical danger.

We consider it a normal reaction if the woman, after coitus and at the peak of satisfaction, embraces the man and presses him to her. We see this as an expression of her gratitude and an affirmation of lasting dependence. But we know it is by no means the rule for a first act of intercourse to lead to such behaviour; in very many cases it is a disappointment for the woman, who remains cold and unsatisfied, and it usually takes more time and frequent repetition of the sexual act before it begins to lead to satisfaction for the woman. A whole series of such cases leads from an initial, fleeting frigidity to the regrettable result of long-term frigidity that cannot be overcome by any efforts of affection on the part of the man. I believe that this frigidity in women has not yet been satisfactorily understood, and apart from cases in which it can be attributed to the unsatisfactory potency of the man, it demands elucidation, possibly with reference to related phenomena.

I do not wish to refer here to those frequent attempts to avoid the first act of sexual intercourse, because they are ambiguous and should be understood primarily, if not wholly, as an expression of universal efforts on the part of women to defend themselves. I believe, on the other hand, that certain pathological cases shed light on the mystery of female frigidity. In these, after the first act, indeed, after every new act of intercourse, the woman manifests her unconcealed hostility towards the man by cursing him, raising her hand to him or actually striking him. In one eminent case of this kind, which I have been able to subject to a detailed analysis, this happened despite the fact that the woman loved the man very much, that it was she herself who tended to demand coitus, and that she clearly derived a high level of satisfaction from it. I think that this strange and contrary reaction is the result of the same impulses that are usually manifested only as frigidity, that is, they are capable of preventing the affectionate reaction without in the process being expressed themselves. In the pathological case, what in frigidity – which occurs far more frequently – is united into an inhibiting effect, is, so to speak, broken down into its two components; this is something we observed long ago in the so-called 'dual-phase' symptoms of compulsive neurosis. According to this theory, the danger thrown up by the defloration of the girl would consist in the fact that one would attract her hostility, and the future husband would have every reason to avoid such enmity.

Analysis easily allows us to guess which of the woman's impulses are involved in the establishment of this paradoxical behaviour, in which I expect to find the explanation of frigidity. The first act of coitus sets in motion a series of such impulses which have no place in the desired feminine attitude, and some of which will not reappear even in later instances of intercourse. We would immediately think of the pain suffered by the virgin during defloration, and we would perhaps be inclined to see that moment as decisive, and desist from looking for others. But we would be wrong in attributing such a meaning to that pain, and should put in its place a narcissistic insult that grows out of the destruction of an organ; this insult finds a rational representation in the knowledge of the diminished sexual value of the deflowered girl herself. The marriage practices of primitive people, however, contain a warning against such over-valuation. We have heard that in some cases the ceremonial occurs in two phases: the rupture of the hymen (with hand or instrument) is followed by an official coitus or a simulacrum of intercourse with the man's representative. This tells us that the significance of the taboo proscription is not fulfilled by the avoidance of anatomical defloration, that the husband should be spared something other than the woman's reaction to the painful injury.

A further reason for disappointment in the first coitus lies in the fact that, for civilized women at least, expectation and fulfilment cannot coincide. Until now, sexual intercourse has been most strongly associated with prohibition, and hence legal and permitted intercourse is not felt to be the same. How deep-seated this connection can be is revealed in an almost comical way by the efforts of so many fiancées to conceal their new amorous relations from all strangers, even from their parents, where there is no need to do so, and no opposition to be feared. The girls say openly that their love will lose value for them if other people know about it. Sometimes this motive can become overpowering, and prevents development of the capacity for love in marriage. The woman can only find her capacity for tender emotions in a forbidden relationship that must remain secret, the only one in which she is sure she will be able to act on the basis of her own will, uninfluenced by anyone else.

However, this motive does not go deep enough either; being linked to civilized conditions, it does not enable us to make a good comparison with the state of affairs among primitive people. More important is the next element, based on the evolution of the libido. The efforts of analysis have enabled us to learn how regular and how powerful the first allocations of the libido are. These concern sexual desires that are preserved from childhood; in women they generally involve fixation of the libido on the father or the brother who takes his place, desires that were often directed at something other than coitus, or included coitus only as a vaguely acknowledged goal. The husband is, so to speak, only ever a substitute, never the right man; someone else, in typical cases the father, has first claim on the woman's capacity for love, the husband has at best the second claim. It now depends how intense that fixation is, and how stubbornly it is maintained, as to whether the substitute man will be rejected as incapable of giving satisfaction. Frigidity is thus subject to the genetic conditions of neurosis. The more powerful the psychical element in the woman's sexual life, the better the distribution of her libido will prove able to withstand the shock of the first sexual act, the less overwhelming physical possession of her will be. Frigidity may then become fixed as a neurotic inhibition, or act as a basis for the development of other neuroses, and even a moderate reduction of the man's potency can supply a great deal of assistance in this process.

The custom of primitive people in transferring the task of defloration to a high elder, a priest, a holy man, a father substitute (see above p. 58–9) seems to take account of an old sexual desire. From here it seems to me to be a simple step to the much-debated *Ius primae noctis* of the medieval lord. A. J. Storfer has defended the same position, and also the widespread institution of 'Tobias nights' (the custom of chastity for the first three nights of marriage) as an acknowledgement of the rights of the patriarch, as C. G. Jung did before him. It thus only confirms our expectations if we encounter the godhead among the father surrogates to whom the task of defloration is entrusted. In some areas of India the newly-wed woman had to sacrifice her hymen to the wooden lingam, and according to St Augustine's account, in the Roman marriage ceremony (of his own time?) the same custom was followed, mitigated by the fact that the young woman had only to sit down on the huge stone phallus of Priapus.

Another motive returns to yet deeper layers, one which demonstrably bears the chief responsibility for the paradoxical reaction against men, and whose influence in my opinion is manifested in the frigidity of women. In women, the first coitus activates yet other impulses than those already described, impulses which resist the feminine function and the feminine role in general.

The analysis of many neurotic women tells us that they pass through an early stage in which they envy their brother the sign of masculinity and, because they lack that sign (although in fact it is only reduced in size), they feel disadvantaged and handicapped. We place this 'penis-envy' under the heading of the 'castration complex'. If we allow 'masculine' to include 'wanting to be masculine', we might apply to such behaviour the term 'masculine protest', coined by

Alfred Adler, to proclaim this factor the bearer of
neurosis in general. During this phase, girls often make
no secret of their envy of their brother, and the enmity
towards him that follows on from it; they even try to
urinate standing up like their brother, as a way of
representing their supposed equality. In the case, mentioned above, of unrestrained post-coital aggression
against an otherwise beloved husband, I was able to
establish that this phase had existed before the object-
choice. Only later on did the little girl's libido turn
towards the father, and then, rather than wishing for
a penis, she wished for – a child.

I should not be surprised if, in other cases too, the
chronological sequence of these impulses were reversed
and this part of the castration complex only came into
effect after the successful object-choice. But the
woman's masculine phase, in which she envies the boy
his penis, is also earlier in terms of the history of
development, and closer to original narcissism than to
object love.

Some time ago I happened to have the opportunity
to study the dream of a newly married woman, which
was recognizable as a reaction to the loss of her virginity. It betrayed without constraint the woman's desire
to castrate the young husband and keep his penis for
herself. Of course there was also room for the more
innocuous interpretation, that she had desired the
act to be prolonged and repeated, only some details
of the dream passed beyond that meaning, and both
the character and the subsequent behaviour of the
dreamer bore out the former interpretation. Behind this

penis-envy there is now revealed the hostile bitterness of the woman towards her husband, which can never quite be ignored in relations between the sexes, and the clearest signs of which are present in the aspirations and literary productions of 'emancipated' women. This hostility on the part of the woman leads Ferenczi – I do not know if he was the first to do this – to engage in palaeobiological speculation about the time when the differentiation of the sexes occurred. At first, he says, copulation took place between two individuals of the same species, one of whom, however, developed into the stronger partner and forced the weaker to endure sexual union. Bitterness over this subjection has survived in the contemporary situation of woman. I do not believe that anyone can be reproached for making use of such speculations, as long as they are careful not to place too much value upon them.

After giving this list of motives for the woman's paradoxical reaction to defloration, traces of which persist in frigidity, we may sum up by saying that the woman's *immature sexuality* is discharged upon the man who first teaches her the sexual act. If that is the case, the virginity taboo is reasonable enough, and we can understand the prescription that the man who is to join in a lasting cohabitation with the woman should avoid such dangers. At higher levels of civilization the appreciation of this danger makes way for the promise of dependence and no doubt for other motives and temptations as well; virginity is held to be a good that the man must not renounce. But the analysis of marital disorders teaches us that those motives which seek to force the woman to avenge herself for her defloration are never entirely extinguished, even from the mental life of the civilized woman. I think it must strike the observer in what seems to be a large number of cases that the woman remains frigid and feels unhappy in a first marriage, while after the dissolution of that marriage she becomes a tender and gratifying wife to her second husband. The archaic reaction has exhausted itself, so to speak, on the first object.

In some other respects, however, the virginity taboo has not completely disappeared from our civilized life. The popular mind is aware of it, and poets have sometimes made use of it. Anzengruber, in a comedy, shows how a simple farmer's boy is held back from marrying the bride meant for him because she is 'a whore that'll cost him 'is life'. For that reason he agrees that someone else should marry her, and he will then take her as a widow, by which time she will have ceased to be dangerous. The title of the play, *Das Jungferngift* [*Virgin's Venom*], recalls the fact that snake-tamers first induce poisonous snakes to bite upon cloths so that they can then handle them unharmed.

The virginity taboo and part of its motivation has its most powerful depiction in Hebbel's tragedy *Judith and Holofernes*. Judith is one of those women whose virginity is protected by a taboo. Her first husband was paralysed by a mysterious anxiety on their wedding night, and did not dare touch her again. 'My beauty is the beauty of deadly nightshade,' she says. 'Enjoyment of it brings madness and death.' When the Assyrian general besieges her city, she devises the plan of seducing and corrupting him with her beauty, employing a patriotic motive to disguise a sexual one. After her defloration by the powerful man, who boasts of his strength and fearlessness, she finds in her rage the strength to cut off his head, and thus becomes the liberator of her people. Decapitation is well known to us as a symbolic substitute for castration; accordingly, Judith is the woman who castrates the man by whom she has been deflowered, as in the dream told to me by the newly married woman. Hebbel has sexualized the patriotic tale from the Apocrypha of the Old Testament with clear intent, because in the biblical account Judith is able, after her return, to boast that she remains unsullied, and the biblical text makes no mention of her sinister wedding night. With the poet's sensitivity, though, he has probably perceived the ancient motif underlying that tendentious story, and only restored the material's older content.

In an excellent analysis, I. Sadger has demonstrated how Hebbel's choice of material was determined by his own parental complex, and how he came so regularly to take the side of woman in the battle of the sexes, empathizing with the hidden impulses of her soul. He also quotes the motivation that the poet himself gave for the changes he had introduced into the material, and rightly finds it specious, seemingly designed outwardly to justify and fundamentally to conceal something of which the poet himself was unconscious. I shall not touch upon Sadger's explanation of why it was necessary for Judith, widowed in the biblical tale, to become a virgin widow. He refers to the intention of the childhood fantasy, disavowing parental sexual intercourse and turning the mother into an intact virgin. But to continue: after the poet had established his heroine's virginity, his sympathetic fantasy persisted in the hostile reaction set off by the violation of her virginity.

In conclusion we may say: defloration does not just have one civilized consequence of binding the woman to the man in a lasting fashion; it also unleashes an archaic reaction of hostility against the man, which can assume pathological forms that are expressed often enough in phenomena of inhibition in marital love-life, and to which we can attribute the fact that second marriages are so often more successful than first ones. The surprising taboo of virginity, and the fear with which, among primitive people, the husband avoids the defloration, find their complete justification in this hostile reaction.

It is interesting, then, that as an analyst one can encounter women in whom the opposite reactions of bondage and enmity are both manifest, and have remained profoundly linked to one another. There are women who seem to have fallen out completely with their husbands, and yet can make only vain attempts to leave them. As soon as they try to turn their love to another man, the image of the first, unloved though he now is, appears as an inhibiting factor between them. Analysis then teaches us that these women are still in a state of bondage with their first husbands, but no longer out of affection. They cannot free themselves from their husbands because they have not yet completed their revenge; in pronounced cases, the vengeful impulse has not even reached consciousness.

On Female Sexuality

During the phase of the normal Oedipus complex, the child is seen as being affectionately attached to the parent of the opposite sex, while hostility predominates in his relations with the parent of the same sex. We have no difficulty in extrapolating from this result where boys are concerned. His mother was the first love object; she remains so, and as his passionate strivings are reinforced and he comes to a deeper understanding of the relationship between father and mother, the father inevitably becomes a rival. Not so where the little girl is concerned. Her first object was also her mother; how can she find her way to her father? How, when and why does she break away from her mother? We have long understood that the development of female sexuality is complicated by the task of relinquishing the originally dominant genital zone, the clitoris, for a new one, the vagina. Now a second such transformation, the exchange of the original object, the mother, for the father, is no less characteristic and significant for woman's development. How the two tasks are connected to one another we cannot yet tell.

As we know, one frequently encounters women who

have strong attachments to their fathers; they are by no means necessarily neurotic. It is among women such as these that I have made the observations that I am reporting here, and which have led me to a particular view of female sexuality. Two facts in particular have struck me about this. The first was: where there was a particularly intense attachment to the father, according to the testimony of the analysis there had previously been a phase of exclusive attachment to the mother, of equal intensity and passion. The second phase had barely added any new features to the patient's love-life apart from a change in object. The primary relationship with the mother had been built up in a very rich and varied way.

The second fact taught us that the duration of this maternal attachment had been greatly underestimated. In several cases it lasted up until the fourth year, in one case until the fifth, and hence it occupied a much longer part of the early blossoming of sexuality than had previously been imagined. Indeed, we had to accept the possibility that a number of females remain frozen in this original maternal attachment, and never really apply it to a man.

The pre-Oedipal phase in women thus attains an importance which we have never previously attributed to it.

Since this phase is able to accommodate all the fixations and repressions to which we trace the origin of the neuroses, it seems necessary to revoke the universality of the thesis that the Oedipus complex is the core of neuroses. But anyone who balks at this correction is not obliged to make it. On the one hand, the Oedipus complex may be extended to encompass all relations between the child and both parents, while on the other, new discoveries may also be taken into account if we say that the woman enters the normal positive Oedipus situation only after overcoming a previous phase governed by the negative complex. During this phase the father is not really much to the girl apart from an annoying rival, although hostility towards him never reaches the characteristic pitch that it does for the boy. We long ago abandoned any expectations of close parallelism between male and female sexual development.

Our insight into the pre-Oedipal early history of the girl comes as a surprise, similar to the revelation, in another field, of the Minoan-Mycenaean culture behind the Greek.

Everything that touches upon this first attachment to the mother seemed to me to be as difficult to grasp analytically, as hoary, shadowy, nearly impossible to revive, as though it had undergone a particularly remorseless repression. Perhaps, though, this impression was due to the fact that women in analysis with me were able to preserve the same attachment to the father, in which they had sought refuge from this earlier phase. In fact, it appears that female analysts like Jeanne Lampl-de Groot and Helene Deutsch have been able to perceive these states of affairs with greater ease and clarity because in their patients the transference to an appropriate mother-substitute was able to take place. Neither have I yet been able to see a case through to its conclusion, so I shall limit myself to communicating results of the most general kind, and give only a few examples of the new insights I have gained. These include the idea that this phase of attachment to the mother is particularly closely connected to the aetiology of hysteria, which can hardly surprise us if we bear in mind that both the phase and the neurosis are among the particular characteristics of femininity, and also that the germ of woman's later paranoia dwells in this dependence on the mother; this seems to be the fear, surprising but regularly encountered, of being killed (devoured?) by the mother. It is natural to assume that this fear corresponds to a hostility towards the mother which develops in the child as a result of the various restrictions of upbringing and physical care, and that the mechanism of projection is encouraged by the fact that psychical organization is in its early stages.

II

I have presented in advance the two facts which have struck me as new: that the woman's strong dependence upon her father only represents the legacy of an equally strong maternal attachment, and that this earlier phase has persisted over an unexpectedly long period of time. Now I should like to go back, to insert these results into the picture of female sexual development with which we are familiar. I will be unable to avoid repeating myself. Our account can only benefit from continuous comparison with the male situation.

First of all, it is unmistakable that the bisexuality claimed for the human constitution is much more clearly present in women than in men. Men, after all, have only one leading sex zone, one sexual organ, while women have two: the actual female vagina and the clitoris, analogous to the male member. We consider ourselves justified in assuming that the vagina is as good as non-existent for many years, and may only supply sensations during puberty. Recently, however, observers have increasingly been suggesting that vaginal impulses also date back to those early years. In girls, therefore, the essential occurrences relating to the genitalia in childhood must take place in the clitoris. The sexual life of women generally divides into two phases, the first of which is male in character; only with the second does it become specifically female. In female development there is thus a process of transport from one phase to the other, and there is nothing analogous to this in men. A further complication arises from the fact that the function of the virile clitoris continues into the later sex life of women, in highly variable ways that we have not satisfactorily understood. Of course we do not know the psychological foundations of these particular qualities in women; even less can we explain their teleological purpose.

Parallel to this first great difference is the difference in the finding of the object. Where the man is concerned, his first love object is his mother, by virtue of the fact that she feeds him and attends to his bodily needs, and she remains so until she is replaced by someone whose nature is similar to her, or derived from her. As to the female concerned, the mother must be her first object too. The primal conditions of object-choice are identical for all children. But by the end of the woman's development the man-father should have become the new love object; that is, the woman's sexual change requires a corresponding change in the sex of the object. New tasks for research arise here, concerning the ways in which this transformation takes place, how thoroughly or incompletely it is accomplished, and what different possibilities arise in this development.

We have already observed that a further difference between the sexes refers to the relationship with the Oedipus complex. It is our impression here that our statement about the Oedipus complex only applies, strictly speaking, to the male child, and that we are right in rejecting the name Electra complex, which seeks to stress the analogy in the behaviour of the two sexes. The fateful relationship of simultaneous love for one parent and a rivalrous hatred for the other only arises in the male child. In him it is then the discovery of the possibility of castration, as proven by the sight of the female genitals, that compels him to transform his Oedipus complex, leads at the same time to the creation of the super-ego, and thus sets in motion all those processes which aim to incorporate the individual within civilized society. Once paternal authority has been internalized into the super-ego, there is a further task which needs to be resolved: the liberation of that authority from the people of whom it was originally a psychical representation. Along this curious path of

development it is precisely the narcissistic genital interest, the one concerned with the preservation of the
penis, that has been turned towards the restriction of
infantile sexuality.

In the man, another remnant of the influence of the
castration complex is a degree of disdain for the
woman, who is recognized as having been castrated.
From this, *in extremis*, an inhibition in object-choice
develops, and with support from organic factors this
can lead to exclusive homosexuality. The effects of the
castration complex are quite different in the woman.
She acknowledges the fact of her castration, and thus
the superiority of the man and her own inferiority,
but she also resists this irksome state of affairs. Three
developmental directions lead off from this contradictory attitude. The first leads to the woman generally
turning away from sexuality. The little girl, alarmed by
comparison with the boy, becomes dissatisfied with
her clitoris, relinquishes her phallic activity and thus
sexuality in general, as well as a good proportion of her
masculinity in other areas. The second direction clings
with defiant self-assertion to her threatened masculinity; the hope of getting another penis is maintained
until an unbelievably late age, it is elevated to a purpose
in life, and the fantasy of being a man in spite of
everything often remains a defining characteristic for
long periods of life. This 'masculinity complex' in the
woman can also issue in a manifestly homosexual
choice of object. It is only the third, very tortuous
path of development that ends up in the final normal
feminine attitude, which chooses the father as its object

and thus arrives at the female form of the Oedipus complex. In women, then, the Oedipus complex is the end result of a longer development, it is not destroyed by the influence of castration, but rather created by it, and it escapes the strong hostile influences that have a destructive effect upon the man; all too often, indeed, the female does not overcome it at all. For this reason the cultural results of its dissolution are also minor and less important. One would probably not be mistaken in saying that it is this difference in the reciprocal relationship between the Oedipus complex and the castration complex that shapes the woman as a social being.

The phase of exclusive attachment to the mother, which may be called *pre-Oedipal*, can thus claim far greater significance in women than it does in men. Many phenomena in female sexual life, which were previously far from accessible to understanding, are completely explained by being traced back to this phase. We have for a long time observed, for example, that many women who have chosen their husband on the model of their father, or put him in the father's place, then repeat in their marriage to him their bad relationship with their mother. The husband is supposed to inherit the relationship with the father, but in fact he inherits the relationship with the mother. That is easily understood as a clear case of regression. The relationship with the mother was the original one, and the attachment to the father was constructed upon it; and now, in marriage, the original relationship emerges out of repression. The transfer of emotional connections from the mother- to the father-object form the chief content of the development leading to womanhood.

If so many women give us the impression that their maturity is filled with quarrels with their husband, just as their youth was spent quarrelling with their mother, in the light of the above observations we will conclude that their hostile attitude towards their mother is not a consequence of the rivalry of the Oedipus complex, but arises from the foregoing phase, and has only been intensified and applied in the Oedipal situation. This is also confirmed by direct analytical examination. We must turn our attention to those mechanisms which have worked to turn the subject away from the maternal object, which was loved so intensely and so exclusively. We are prepared to find not one such element but a whole series of elements, working together towards the same final goal.

Among these some emerge which arise from the conditions of infantile sexuality in general, and which thus apply equally well to the erotic life of boys. First among these we should mention jealousy of other people, of brothers and sisters, rivals, also allowing room for the father. Children's love is boundless, it demands exclusivity, it is not satisfied with scraps. But a second characteristic of this love is that in reality it also has no goal, it is incapable of complete satisfaction, and for that reason it is to a large extent condemned to end in disappointment and make way for an attitude of hostility. In later life the absence of final satisfaction may favour a different outcome. As in erotic relationships in which the goal is inhibited, this element may ensure the undisturbed continuation of libidinal investment, but under the compulsion of developmental processes the libido regularly abandons the unsatisfying position in order to seek a new one.

Another much more specific motive for turning away from the mother emerges from the effect of the castration complex upon the creature without a penis. At some point the little girl discovers her organic inferiority, and she naturally does this earlier and more easily if she has brothers or if there are other boys near by. We have already heard of the three paths that part in that case: *a)* one leads towards the cessation of the whole of the sexual life; *b)* one leads towards the defiant over-emphasis of masculinity; *c)* one leads towards the beginnings of a final femininity. It is not easy to make more precise statements concerning time, or to establish typical modes of evolution. The moment of the discovery of castration is itself variable, and other elements appear to be inconstant and dependent on chance. The condition of the girl's own phallic activity also comes into consideration, along with the question of whether or not it has been discovered, and, if it has been, what level of prohibition has been imposed upon it.

In most cases the little girl spontaneously finds her own phallic activity, clitoral masturbation, and it is at first practised without a fantasy. The frequently occurring fantasy that turns the mother, nurse or nanny into a seducer is due to the influence of bodily care upon the first awakening of this activity. Whether masturbation among girls is rarer and, from the start, less energetic than among boys is an open question; it is certainly possible. Real seduction, too, is frequently enough, whether by other children or carers who wish to calm the child down, send her to sleep or make her dependent upon them. Where seduction is involved, it generally disturbs the natural course of developmental processes; it often has far-reaching and lasting consequences.

As we have heard, the prohibition on masturbation becomes a reason for abandoning the practice, but it is also a reason to rebel against the person imposing the prohibition, the mother, or the mother-substitute, who generally merges with the mother later on. The defiant assertion of masturbation seems to open the way to masculinity. Even where the child has not succeeded in suppressing masturbation, the outcome of the seemingly ineffectual prohibition becomes apparent in her later efforts to free herself, at the cost of greater sacrifices, from the satisfaction that has been spoiled for her. Even the object-choice of the adolescent girl can be influenced by the persistence of this intention. Rancour over the prevention of free sexual activity plays a major part in separation from the mother. The same motive will once again come into effect after puberty, when the mother recognizes her duty to protect her daughter's modesty. We will not, of course, forget that the mother takes similar steps against her son's masturbation, and thus gives him, too, a strong motive for rebellion.

If the little girl experiences her own deficiency as the

result of seeing the male genitals, she does not accept this undesirable information without hesitation or resistance. As we have heard, she stubbornly clings to the expectation that she will herself at some point acquire such a set of genitals, and the desire for this to happen survives the hope for a long time. In all cases the child initially sees castration as an individual misfortune, and only later does it extend that misfortune to individual children, and finally to individual adults. When the child comes to understand the universality of this negative characteristic, the result is a great devaluation of femininity, and hence of the mother.

It is entirely possible that the above description of the little girl's response to the impression of castration and the prohibition on masturbation will make a confused and contradictory impression on the reader. That is not entirely the fault of the author. In fact, it is barely possible to produce an account that is universally applicable. We encounter the most diverse reactions, and contradictory attitudes can exist side by side in a single individual. The first imposition of the prohibition creates a conflict which will henceforward accompany the development of the sexual function. Comprehension of this idea is made even harder by the efforts involved in distinguishing the mental processes of this first phase from later phases, which cover it over and distort it in the memory. Thus, for example, the fact of castration is understood as a punishment for masturbatory activity, but its execution is transferred to the father; two things that must certainly not be original. The boy, too, generally fears castration by his father, although the threat is usually expressed by his mother.

Be that as it may, it is at the end of this first phase of attachment to the mother that the strongest motive for turning away from her appears, in the notion that she has not given the child proper genitals; which is to say that she has given birth to the child as a female. One is not surprised to hear another accusation with a rather shorter history: the mother has given the child too little milk, and not nursed it for long enough. In our cultural conditions that may often be the case, but it is certainly not true as often as is claimed in analysis. It seems rather that this accusation is an expression of universal dissatisfaction among children, who are, under the cultural conditions of monogamy, weaned off the breast after six to nine months – whereas primitive mothers devote themselves exclusively to their child for two to three years – as though our children were to remain unsatisfied for ever, as though they had never sucked long enough on their mother's breast. But I am not sure whether one would encounter the same complaint in the analysis of children who were nursed for as long as the children of primitive people. So great is the appetite of the child's libido! If we consider the whole series of motivations uncovered by analysis for turning away from the mother: that she neglected to equip the girl with the only correct form of genitals, that she fed her inadequately and forced her to share maternal love with others, that she never fulfilled all the expectations of love, and finally that she first stimulated and then prohibited the girl's sexual activity –

none of these motivations seems adequately to justify the final hostility. Some are inevitable consequences of the nature of infantile sexuality, others are distinguished as later rationalizations of an emotional change that has not been understood. Perhaps it is truer to say that the attachment to the mother is doomed to collapse precisely because it is the first and because it is so intense, as we can often observe in the first marriages of young women which occurred when they were very much in love. I would suggest that in both cases the attitude of love can be seen to fail because of the inevitable disappointments and the accumulation of causes for aggression. Second marriages are generally more successful.

We cannot go so far as to claim that the ambivalence of emotional investments is a universally valid psychological law, that it is in general impossible to feel great love for a person without the addition of a hatred that may be equally great, or vice versa. There is no doubt that the normal person, the adult, manages to keep the two attitudes separate, not hating the object of his love or loving his enemy. But that seems to be the result of later developments. During the first phase of erotic life ambivalence is clearly the rule. In many people this archaic trait is preserved throughout the whole of life, and it is characteristic of compulsive neurotics that love and hatred are kept in balance in their object relations. We may assert the predominance of ambivalence among primitive people, too. The little girl's intense attachment to her mother must therefore also be highly ambivalent, and, with the help of other elements, it must, because of this very ambivalence, be forced away from the mother; once again, then, this is down to a universal characteristic of infantile sexuality.

Against this attempt at explanation a question immediately arises: how is it possible for boys to hold on to their attachment to their mother, which is certainly no less intense? We also have a ready answer to that question: it is because they have been enabled to deal with their ambivalence towards their mother by placing all their hostile emotions upon their father. First, though, we should not give this answer without having thoroughly studied the pre-Oedipal phase in boys; and secondly it would probably be more prudent to admit to ourselves that we have not gained a complete understanding of these processes, of which we have just become aware.

III

One further question is: What does the little girl demand from her mother? Of what nature are her sexual goals during the period of the exclusive attachment to the mother? The answer that we draw from the analytical material accords completely with our expectations. The girl's sexual goals as regards her mother are both active and passive in nature, and they are defined by the phases of the libido through which the child passes. In this context the relationship between activity and passivity deserves our particular interest. We may easily observe that in every area of mental experience, and not only that of sexuality, a passively received impression in the child provokes an active reaction. The child itself tries to do what has in the past been done to it. This is a task involving the mastery of the external world that has been imposed upon the child, and it can even lead to the child attempting to repeat impressions that it would have cause to avoid because of their painful content. Children's play serves this intention of complementing a passive experience with an active action, as a way, we might say, of abolishing it. If the doctor has opened the mouth of the resisting child to look into its throat, after the doctor has left the child will act out his role, repeating the violent procedure with its little sister, who is just as helpless towards the child as the child was to the doctor. It is impossible not to see this as a rejection of passivity and a preference of the active role. This swing from passivity to activity does not occur equally regularly and energetically in all children, and in some it may not happen at all. From this behaviour in the child we may draw conclusions about the relative strength of masculinity and femininity that it will manifest in its sexuality.

The child's first sexual, or sexually tinged, experiences with its mother are naturally passive in nature. It is by the mother that the child is suckled, fed, cleaned, dressed and guided in everything it does. Part of the child's libido persists in these experiences and enjoys the satisfactions connected with them, while another part tries to convert them into activity. Being nursed at the mother's breast is replaced by active sucking of the breast. In other respects the child contents itself either with autonomy, that is, by accomplishing on its own something that was previously done to it, or by actively repeating its passive experiences in play; or else it will actually make the mother its object, behaving towards her as an active subject. This last kind of behaviour, which occurs in the field of actual activity, seemed incredible to me for a long time until experience refuted my doubts.

We seldom hear of a little girl wanting to wash or dress her mother, or instructing her to perform her excretory functions. Certainly, the girl will sometimes say: 'Now let's play me being the mother and you being the child' – but more usually she fulfils these active desires indirectly, in play with her doll, with herself representing the mother as the doll represents the child. The fact that girls, unlike boys, prefer to play with dolls, is usually taken as a sign that femininity has awoken early. And that would not be a mistake, but we should not ignore the fact that it is the active side of femininity that is being manifested here, and that this preference on the part of the girl probably testifies to the passivity of the attachment to the mother, to the complete neglect of the father-object.

The highly surprising sexual activity of the girl towards the mother is expressed chronologically in oral, sadistic and finally even in phallic efforts directed at her. It is difficult to give an account of the details, because they are often obscure drive impulses which the child was unable to grasp psychically when they occurred, which have therefore been interpreted only retrospectively, and which then appear in analysis in modes of expression that they would certainly not originally have possessed. Sometimes we encounter these as transferences to the later father-object, where they should not be and where they severely obstruct understanding. We encounter aggressive oral and sadistic desires in the form into which they were compelled by early repression, as a fear of being killed by the mother which in turn justifies a desire for the mother's death if the desire becomes conscious. We cannot tell how often this fear of the mother is supported by unconscious hostility on the mother's part, and guessed by the child. (Hitherto I have only ever encountered the fear of being eaten among men; it is linked to the father, but it probably results from the transformation of oral aggression directed at the mother. One wants to devour the mother from whom one has been fed; in the case of the father the immediate cause for this desire is absent.)

People of the female sex who have a strong attachment to their mother, and whose pre-Oedipal phase I have been able to study, are agreed in stating that they showed the greatest resistance to the enemas that their mother performed upon them, reacting with fear and cries of rage. This may be a very common or even a universal form of behaviour among children. I acquired my understanding of the explanation of this particularly violent resistance from an observation by Ruth Mack Brunswick, who was dealing with the same problems at the same time, in which she sought to compare the outbreak of fury after an enema to orgasm after genital stimulation. The anxiety aroused in this context would then be understood as a translation of the pleasure in aggression stimulated by these injections. I believe that this is in fact the case, and that during the sadistic/anal stage the response to the intense passive stimulation of the colonic zone is an outbreak of aggression, which presents itself directly as rage or, when suppressed, as anxiety. This reaction seems to cease in later years.

Among the passive impulses of the phallic phase, one stands out: the girl regularly accuses the mother of being a seducer because she has felt her first or strongest genital sensations when her mother (or her substitute, a carer) was cleaning her and tending to her bodily functions. Mothers, from observation of their two- to three-year-old daughters, have often told me that the child enjoys these sensations and requires the mother to intensify them with repeated contact and rubbing. It is, I believe, because the mother so inevitably inaugurates the child's phallic phase that in the fantasies of later years it is the father who so regularly appears as the sexual seducer. In the act of turning away from the mother the introduction into sexual life has been transferred to the father.

Finally, during the phallic phase, there arise intense active impulses of desire directed towards the mother. Sexual activity during this period culminates in masturbation with the clitoris, probably while the mother is being imagined, but my experience would not enable me to guess whether the child is imagining a sexual goal, or what that goal might be. Such a goal can be clearly discerned only when the interests of the child have been given fresh impetus by the arrival of a little brother or sister. The little girl claims to have given the mother this new child, just as the boy does, and her reaction to this event and her behaviour towards the child are identical. That sounds fairly absurd, but perhaps only because it sounds so unfamiliar to us.

The fact that the girl turns away from the mother is an extremely significant step along her path of development, and it is more than a mere change of object. We have already described its source and its many supposed motivations; we shall now add that hand in hand with it we may observe a pronounced decline in active, and a rise in passive sexual impulses. Certainly, active strivings are more strongly affected by frustration, they have proved entirely incapable of accomplishment, and for that reason they are also more easily abandoned by the libido, but at the same time there has been no shortage of disappointments on the passive side. Clitoral masturbation often begins as the girl turns away from her mother, and in many cases, when the little girl's earlier masculinity is repressed, lasting damage is done to a great proportion of her sexual striving. The transition to the father-object is completed with the help of passive strivings, where these have escaped disaster. The path towards the development of femininity is now opened to the girl, in so far as it is not obstructed by the residues of the pre-Oedipal attachment to the mother, now overcome.

If we now survey the phase of female sexual development described above, we cannot avoid making a certain judgement about femininity as a whole. We have found the same libidinal forces at work here as in the male child, and have been able to convince ourselves that for a while they both take the same paths and attain the same results.

Then it is biological factors that distract them from their original goals, and guide even active strivings, masculine in every sense, on to the tracks of femininity. As we cannot help attributing sexual excitement to the effect of certain chemical substances, we may expect that biochemistry will one day offer us a substance whose presence provokes masculine sexual excitement, and one that provokes female sexual excitement. But this hope seems no less naïve than the hope, fortunately now a thing of the past, that one might discover stimuli for hysteria, compulsive neurosis, melancholy and so on individually under the microscope.

More complicated factors must also be at work in sexual chemistry. For psychology, however, it is irrelevant whether the body contains a single sexually stimulating substance, or two, or a huge number. Psychoanalysis teaches us to get by with a single libido, albeit one which has active and passive goals or types of satisfaction. It is in this opposition, and above all in the existence of libidinous strivings with passive goals, that the rest of the problem is contained.

IV

If we study the analytic literature about our subject, we will be convinced that everything I have presented here is already contained within it. There would have been no need to publish this work if, in an area so difficult of access, it was not always valuable to give an account of one's own experiences and personal conceptions. I myself have attained a keener understanding of things, and have isolated them more carefully. In some other studies, the exposition cannot be grasped all at once because of the simultaneous discussion of the problems of guilt and the super-ego. I have avoided that, and in the description of the various outcomes of this phase of development I have not examined the complications that result if the child, following the disappointment with her father, returns to the abandoned attachment to her mother, or throughout the course of her life switches repeatedly between one attitude and the other. But precisely because my work is only one contribution among others, I may spare myself an in-depth appraisal of the literature, and can limit myself to stressing significant agreements with some of these works and important deviations from others.

In Abraham's currently unsurpassed description of the 'Äusserungsformen des weiblichen Kastrationskomplexes' ['Manifestations of the Female Castration Complex'], (*Internationale Zeitschrift für Psychoanalyse*, VII, 1921), one would like the element of the initially exclusive attachment to the mother to have been included. I must agree with the essential points in the important work of Jeanne Lampl-de Groot. This author acknowledges the complete identity of the pre-Oedipal phase in boys and girls, asserts the sexual (phallic) activity of the girl in regard to her mother, and proves it through observations. She traces the turning-away from the mother back to the influence of the knowledge of castration, which forces the child to renounce its sexual object and thus, in many cases, masturbation as well; she has expressed the overall development in the formula that the girl passes through a phase of 'negative' Oedipus complex, before she can enter the positive one. I see one shortcoming of this work in that it portrays turning away from the mother as a mere change of object, and does not take into account the fact that it is accomplished amid clear indications of hostility. This hostility is fully appreciated in the final work of Helene Deutsch ('Der feminine Masochismus und seine Beziehung zur Frigidität' ['Feminine Masochism and its Relation to Frigidity'], *Internationale Zeitschrift für Psychoanalyse*, XVI, 1930), which acknowledges the girl's phallic activity and the intensity of her attachment to her mother. Helene Deutsch also states that the act of turning towards the father also occurs via passive strivings (which have already been aroused in relation to the mother). In her earlier (1925) published book *Psychoanalyse der weiblichen Sexualfunktionen* [*Psychoanalysis of Female Sexual Functions*] she had not yet dispensed with application of the Oedipal scheme, and therefore interpreted the girl's phallic activity as identification with the father.

Fenichel ('Zur prägenitalen Vorgeschichte des Ödipuskomplexes' ['On the Pre-genital History of the Oedipus Complex'], *Internationale Zeitschrift für Psychoanalyse*, XVI, 1930) correctly stresses the difficulty of identifying, from the material thrown up by analysis, the content from the pre-Oedipal phase that persists unaltered in it, and which has been regressively (or otherwise) distorted. He does not acknowledge the girl's phallic activity as identified by Jeanne Lampl-de Groot, and also protests against the 'precipitation' of the Oedipus complex undertaken by Melanie Klein ('Frühstadien des Ödipuskonfliktes' ['Early Stages of the Oedipus Conflict'], *Internationale Zeitschrift für Psychoanalyse* XIV, 1928 and elsewhere), which she shifts back to the beginning of the second year. This temporal definition, which inevitably also changes the conception of all other relations of development, does not in fact coincide with the results of the analysis of adults, and is particularly difficult to reconcile with my findings about the girl's lengthy pre-Oedipal attachment to the mother. One way of mitigating this contradiction lies in the observation that in this field we cannot yet distinguish between that which is rigidly established by biological laws and that which is mobile and changeable under the influence of accidental experience. As we have long known with regard to the effect of seduction, other elements – the time of the birth of brothers and sisters, the time of the discovery of sexual difference, the direct observation of sexual intercourse, the encouraging or prohibiting attitude of the parents, and so on – can provoke an acceleration and maturing of child sexual development.

Some authors are inclined to play down the significance of the child's first and most original libidinal impulses in favour of later developmental processes, so that the role of these impulses – *in extremis* – is only to indicate certain directions, while the psychical intensities that follow those paths are supplied by later regressions and reaction-formations; thus, for example, when K. Horney ('Flucht aus der Weiblichkeit' [Flight from Womanhood], *Internationale Zeitschrift für Psychoanalyse*, XII, 1926) says that we greatly underestimate the girl's primary penis-envy, while the intensity of the later striving towards masculinity should be attributed to a secondary penis-envy, which is used to send off feminine impulses, particularly the feminine attachment to the father. That does not correspond to my impressions. However certain the presence of later reinforcements produced through regression and reaction-formation may be, however difficult it may be to undertake a relative assessment of the converging components of the libido, I do not think we should ignore the fact that those first libidinal impulses have an intensity of their own which remains greater than all later impulses, and which we may actually call incommensurable. It is certainly correct to say that an opposition exists between attachment to the father and the masculinity complex – it is the general opposition between activity and passivity, masculinity and femininity – but that does not give us the right to assume that one alone is primary, and the other owes its strength only to resistance. And if resistance to femininity occurs so energetically, whence can it derive its force but from the striving for masculinity, which is first manifested in the child's penis-envy and therefore deserves to be named after it?

A similar objection can be made to Jones's conception ('Die erste Entwicklung der weiblichen Sexualität' ['The Early Development of Female Sexuality'], *Internationale Zeitschrift für Psychoanalyse*, VIII, 1927), according to which the phallic stage in girls is more of a secondary protective reaction than a real stage of development. This corresponds neither to dynamic nor to temporal conditions.

(1931)